The Historic Haile Homestead at Kanapaha Plantation: An Illustrated History

by

Karen Kirkman and Kevin McCarthy

Historic Haile Homestead, Inc.

2014

ISBN-13:978-1500650421

ISBN-10:1500650420

All proceeds from the sale of this book will go to the Historic Haile Homestead Inc., the 501(c)3 non-profit organization which operates and preserves the Historic Haile Homestead.

This book is dedicated to all the passionate volunteers who have helped and continue to work tirelessly to preserve and operate the Historic Haile Homestead.

The Historic Haile Homestead, Inc. is registered with the State of Florida to solicit contributions. A copy of the official registration and financial information may be obtained from the Division of Consumer Services by calling toll-free (800-435-7352) within the state. Registration does not imply endorsement, approval, or recommendation by the State of Florida.

For more information about the Historic Haile Homestead, please visit www.hailehomestead.org. Membership and docent information is found under How To Help. Or visit www.facebook.com/hailehomestead Mailing address: Historic Haile Homestead Inc. 4941 SW 91st Terrace, Suite 101, Gainesville, Florida 32608. Physical address: 8500 SW Archer Road, Gainesville, Florida 32608. Phone: (352) 336-9096.

Email address: hailedocent@yahoo.com

Table of Contents

Acknowledgements

First and foremost I would like to thank my co-author, Dr. Kevin McCarthy, for suggesting we write this book together. In the midst of several volunteer projects and managing the day-to-day operations of the Homestead, it would have been easy to decline for lack of free time. But Kevin and my friend Hank Conner convinced me it was the right thing to do at the right time. So here we are. This book would not have been possible without the support of the Haile family: Graham Haile, Evans Haile, Bev Haile Parrish, and Nancy Haile Bowden. Special thanks to Graham and Evans for sharing so many memories and old photos. Thanks also go to many other Haile descendants for their stories, pictures, and artifacts, especially Mary Chesnut Budd Gearing, Mary Budd Holmes, J.D. Henry, Hunter Davis, Ann Davis, Henrietta Vinson, and Peggy Haile Thomas (decd). Many thanks to others who contributed either research, reflections or answered many questions either for this book or for the body of information we have accumulated over time: Lamar Taylor, Jay Reeves, Murray Laurie, Jim Powell Jr., Isaiah Branton, Dr. Patricia Hilliard-Nunn, Melanie Barr, Barbara Stringfellow, Jim Stringfellow, Dr. Lucy Wayne, Martin Dickinson, Robert Hutchinson, Miles Gardner of Kershaw, SC, Linda White at the Haile Gold Mine, Kershaw SC, Marty Daniels of Mulberry Plantation, Camden SC, and Dr. Bruce Brown of the Bloomsbury Inn, Camden, SC. Please forgive any omissions as there have been so many people who have shared with us over the years. Finally, my most heartfelt gratitude is reserved for my family, my husband Mike, and our sons Nate and Ryan, and my best friend Kaley Behl, who have supported me, encouraged me and tolerated many side trips to old houses, libraries, and cemeteries. These are the people who keep me going. Thank you.

Introduction

Just west of Gainesville, Florida, lies an archaeological/historical gem: the Historic Haile Homestead. "Kanapaha," was the home of Thomas Evans Haile and Esther "Serena" Chesnut Haile and 14 of their fifteen children. On that site in the center of about forty acres is a house dating back to the mid-19th century that not only shows what life was like for early white settlers, but also how a plantation functioned with enslaved laborers. What is also unique at the site is something that the knowledgeable docents call "Talking Walls," well-preserved writings on the actual interior walls that include recipes, poems, reminders about taking medicine, lists of party guests, and even a caricature of a U.S. president. One docent copied down more than 12,500 words from the walls.

Those forty acres at the household site are all that remain from an original 1500 acres. Visitors driving by on S.R. 24/Archer Road cannot see the magnificent house from the road, but – for those who make the effort to stop and visit and ask questions – a whole new world opens up, a world of 19th- and early 20th-century plantation life. The well-preserved house, surrounded by lush foliage and a few remnants of the former life there, has begun telling us its secrets because of the careful, meticulous research by historians, anthropologists, and archaeologists.

In fact the Historic Haile Homestead is one of the very few remaining antebellum homes in north-central Florida. The Haile family, which still owns a half interest in the property, and the Alachua Conservation Trust (ACT), which owns the other half, initiated a restoration of the house and grounds in the early 1990s. The restoration was funded by a grant from the State of Florida. The partnership between the Hailes and ACT allowed them to get the grant.

A view of the front porch and one side of the house

The Historic Haile Homestead is open for tours on a regular basis, allowing visitors an opportunity to take a step back in time and experience life in Florida as it was during the mid-1800s to the early 1900s. Visitors to the site should consult its web site (http://www.hailehomestead.org/) for more information about tours and events.

Chapter One: Prehistory to 1512

Thousands of years ago the climate of the world differed dramatically from today's weather. Large glaciers covered about one-fourth of the earth, including the top half of the present-day United States, and much of the world's water was frozen in glaciers. The level of the oceans was much lower than it is today, by as much as 350 feet.

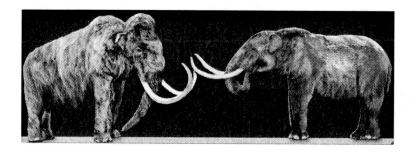

A mammoth (on the left) and a mastodon

At a time when Asia and North America were joined at the Bering Strait west of present-day Alaska, about fifty thousand years ago, hunters made their way across that land-bridge looking for animals like the giant mastodon and mammoth.

Those intrepid hunters spread out over North America and settled in places where they could fish and hunt for animals like the mastodon, mammoth, and giant ground sloth.

Paleontologists working throughout Florida, including Alachua County, have found the bones of such animals and have given them to museums, including the Museum of Natural History in Gainesville, for visitors to see and better understand what giant animals once roamed our area.

1

Paleontologists have found the remains of some of those animals in present-day Alachua County. Open-pit quarrying at the Haile quarries 15 miles west of Gainesville has revealed specimens from the Pleistocene Epoch (from about 2,588,000 to 11,700 years ago) and the Early Miocene Epoch (23 million to 16 million years ago).

In Gilchrist County, northwest of the Haile site, is the Thomas Farm site, which paleontologists have been excavating for over eight decades – impressive finds that include bears, and bear-dogs, camels, dogs, and three-toed horses.

About twelve thousand years ago, some of the people who migrated from Asia reached Florida in what is called the Paleoindian Period. The Paleoindians hunted, fished, ate wild plants, and spent much of their time just trying to survive. Archaeologists have found in rivers and springs some of the weapons that those early Floridians used to hunt and fish. In the illustration below, notice the three "deer" on the left of the stream, deer that are actually disguised Native Americans with bows and arrows.

The image here was originally an engraving published by European engraver Theodor de Bry in 1591. He based this and other engravings on watercolors done by Jacques Le Moyne de Morgues, a French artist who accompanied French explorer Jean Ribault's 1564 expedition to Florida.
The illustrations are the earliest-known European depictions of Native Americans in what is today the United States.

The image on the previous page of the Indians hunting deer near water may remind us of Lake Kanapaha, a freshwater body of water about a mile east of the Haile Homestead. Archaeologists have determined that Timucuan Indians once lived at the lake. According to *Florida Place Names* by Allen Morris, the word "Kanapaha" derives from the Timucuan words *cani* "palmetto leaves" and *paha* "house," referring to the large structures of poles thatched with bark or palmetto bark.

Though the last syllable of "Kanapaha" is most often pronounced as "ha," some family members substitute "haw" on the end, possibly the way Thomas and Serena Haile pronounced it. That lake was near enough to the Haile Homestead that the family used it for fishing, as is clear from the diary kept by Serena Haile.

A pond near Lake Kanapaha, which is totally dried up today

One of the rooms at the Haile Homestead has a display of arrowheads a local man found, but exactly where is unknown. We do know the Indians attacked their prey at watering holes, including lakes and rivers.

As time went on and the large animals became extinct, the Indians settled either near the coasts to fish or inland, where they could farm the land. Many Indians relied on freshwater fish from the peninsula's lakes, ponds, and rivers, as well as the oysters and clams they could find in estuaries.

3

The size of Florida may have been twice as large as it is today since much of the world's water was stored in glaciers, and ocean levels were much lower. In fact, this Florida peninsula stretched far out into the Gulf of Mexico. About nine thousand years ago, the climate of the world warmed considerably, the glaciers melted, and the level of the oceans rose, reducing the size of many coastal lands, including Florida.

Indian games like the ones pictured in these 16th-century engravings might have been performed in what is today Alachua County.

Those Indian sites that were inundated by the Gulf of Mexico and the Atlantic Ocean may have been lost forever, but the Indians who were resourceful and far-thinking no doubt adapted to the new geography and moved inland.

Present-day Alachua County would not be as affected by that shrinkage of the peninsula as would be the coastal sites.

Chapter Two: 1513 to 1699

The Arrival of European Explorers in Florida

Long before the Spanish arrived in La Florida in 1513, Native Americans lived here, fishing the waters, hunting the prairies, and raising their families. Anthropologists call the Native Americans who lived in what is today Alachua County the Timucuans.

In 1513, Ponce de León led the first group of European explorers to Florida, landing someplace on the east coast of La Florida. In 1565, Pedro Menéndez de Avilés landed in northeast Florida and established St. Augustine.

One Spanish explorer who might have gone through what today is Alachua County was Hernando de Soto, who landed in Tampa Bay in 1539 with over six hundred men, including priests, farmers, merchants, and craftsmen.

Hernando de Soto

They traveled north through Ocala and present-day Alachua County, but their precise route is unclear.

The expedition traveled through the southeastern United States for three years before de Soto died in 1542 near the Mississippi River.

5

Around 1600, the Spanish established missions among the Indians, sometimes with full-time resident priests. As described in such works as Michael Gannon's *The Cross in the Sand: The Early Catholic Church in Florida, 1513 – 1870*, the Franciscan missionaries set up missions to convert Native Americans to Catholicism and to teach them to cultivate crops – with some success in each endeavor.

However, while Catholic missionaries usually treated the Native Americans well, some of the Spanish explorers did not, but instead forced them into slavery and menial work constructing ranches, forts, and buildings. And so, the relations between Native Americans and Europeans deteriorated in the latter half of the 16th century and into the 17th century as the powerful weapons and diseases of the Europeans decimated the indigenous population.

*A depiction of how European diseases exacted
a heavy toll among the Native Americans*

The Indians did not have a written language, but we know much about them from the reports of Spanish explorers and missionaries.

Chapter Three: 1700 to 1799

In the 1700s, a group of Native Americans, the Creeks, split off from the Lower Creek Indians in present-day Georgia and Alabama and headed south to Florida. They were seeking new lands to cultivate and found the Timucuans in Florida were growing fewer because of the effects of European diseases, slavery by the Spanish, and losses from battles with other Indians. The Creeks joined with other Native Americans, the Yamasee, and attacked the remaining Timucuans, who were forced to seek help from the Spanish, but the latter enslaved them.

At that time, only a few thousand white settlers were living in the peninsula, mostly around St. Augustine. The Creeks assimilated many of the Native Americans in Florida and headed even further south in the peninsula. Europeans called the new group "Seminoles," from the word "cimarrones," a word meaning "runaways, wild ones." Among the new immigrants to La Florida were escaped slaves from southern colonies.

Some of those slaves joined the Native Americans and were known as Black Seminoles. In general, the St. Johns River formed the boundary between Europeans to the east of the river and Native Americans to the west of the river.

Black Seminoles like Negro Abraham, pictured here in the 1830s, became valuable allies of the Seminoles because the former knew English, having worked on slave plantations in the South.

7

In 1763, the Spanish ceded Florida to the British, who would nominally rule the territory for the next twenty years. Among the British visitors to Florida during that two-decade time period was a young man from Philadelphia, William Bartram (1739 – 1823), who accompanied his father, John Bartram (1699 – 1777), to the South, including Florida.

Their purpose was to collect plant specimens to send back to a botanist in England. The King of England had appointed John Bartram the official botanist in the New World and the founder of the first North American botanical garden (1728). His son, William, returned to Florida, visited different places in north-central Florida, including Alachua County, and befriended the Indians there.

The descriptions of the flora and fauna of north-central Florida, as written by William Bartram (pictured to the right), inspired other British writers, for example William Wordsworth and Samuel Taylor Coleridge.

In 1784 Spain regained Florida from England and began the Second Spanish Period (1784 – 1821), but had too few soldiers and settlers to make any real claim on the territory. During that time, lawlessness prevailed, and a wide variety of settlers moved in, including runaway slaves, Creek Indians, and white adventurers looking for cheap land. In addition to all of that, fervent patriots wanted the United States to annex the peninsula away from all the European powers and thus open up the land to expansion by the fledgling American government.

Chapter Four: 1800 to 1809

During the Second Spanish Period (1784 – 1821), Spanish control over Florida gradually diminished. More Native Americans moved into the peninsula, and American residents who were just north of the border continued to agitate for an American takeover of the land.

Because relatively few Spanish merchants were willing to settle in Florida, Spanish authorities allowed non-Spanish firms to do business. One of those was a British firm, Panton, Leslie and Company, which had operated during the British occupation (1763 – 1783), to trade with the Native Americans of Florida, supplying them with munitions, alcohol, and other goods in exchange for deerskins, furs, honey, and foodstuffs.

The old Panton, Leslie & Company warehouse in Pensacola

North-central Florida, where the Hailes would settle in the 1850s, had many more white settlers than South Florida, something that would be dramatically altered in the twentieth century. Even so, the frontier conditions of the peninsula attracted only the hardier immigrants. What did attract settlers, whether Seminole Indians or people from Georgia looking for new opportunities, was the mild but varied climate of North Florida and the rich, fertile lands in the area that could be used for planting crops or raising cattle.

One of the most unusual white settlers in Florida in this time period was William Augustus Bowles (1763 or 1764 – 1805), a white man who had come to Florida from Maryland at the age of twelve, lived with the Indians, and married the daughter of an Indian chief. While attempting to organize the Native Americans of Florida, he was twice imprisoned by the Spanish and eventually died while imprisoned in Cuba's Morro Castle in 1805.

William Augustus Bowles

Meanwhile, Camden, where the Hailes would come from, developed as an important inland trade center in the colony of South Carolina.

During the American Revolution (1765 – 1783), when the thirteen original colonies broke away from the British Empire and became the United States of America, Camden was the scene of the worst American defeat of the war.

In 1780, British troops under Lord Charles Cornwallis established in Camden a major supply center for the British in the South. At the Battle of Camden in 1780, the British defeated the American troops, but at the Battle of Hobkirk Hill the following year the American troops, under General Nathanael Greene, although defeated, forced the British to retreat to the coast.

After the war, Camden thrived as a trading town and as a center for growing cotton, a crop that was dependent on good soil and plentiful rain.

Chapter Five: 1810 to 1819

The second decade of the 19th century saw renewed Spanish efforts to keep control of Florida, efforts that would end in the next decade. In 1812, U.S. officials sent former Georgia governor George Mathews into Spanish Florida to try to convince more American settlers to move there and resist the Spanish. However, as the U.S. was preparing for the War of 1812 against England, it did not want another front with Spain and therefore sent American troops into La Florida to maintain some kind of peace there.

The desperate Spanish, knowing that they were vastly outnumbered by American troops willing to fight to control this peninsula, tried to enlist the aid of the Seminole Indians against the Americans – with mixed results. Some of the Indians, e.g. an Indian leader named Payne (after whom Paynes Prairie would be named), refused, but Payne's younger half-brother, Bowlegs, sided with the Spanish and convinced other Seminoles to attack American settlers around St. Augustine and along the St. Johns River.

A modern resident of Paynes Prairie Preserve State Park,
the Florida alligator

Those Indian attacks against American settlers angered other Americans throughout the South. In September 1812, a Georgia militia colonel, Daniel Newnan, led a troop of 117 volunteers into Florida and attacked the Seminoles at Paynes Town near today's Micanopy. In a pitched battle near the town, the Seminoles warded off the white troops and drove them back north, eventually to Georgia. At least sixteen of the white troops were killed, while some fifty Seminoles were killed, including Payne himself.

Colonel Newnan (1780 – 1851) later served as the superintendent of the Georgia State Penitentiary, Secretary of State of Georgia, and a congressional representative in the U.S. Congress. He is honored in the naming of Newnan, Georgia, and in two places in Alachua County, Florida, despite his relatively minor effect on the history of this area: the county's first seat of government (Newnansville) and the large lake to the east of Gainesville (Newnan's Lake). Occasionally, local historians, knowing that Native Americans lived in the area for hundreds of years, try to restore the original Indian name of the lake, Pithlachocco, but to no avail.

The fishing pier at Pithlachocco or Newnan's Lake near Gainesville

One reason the Hailes probably did not encounter any Native Americans when the former came to Alachua County in the 1850s was what occurred several decades earlier in Florida: the Seminole Indian Wars.

After the War of 1812, slave owners suspected that many of their escaped slaves had headed south to Florida, where the Spanish offered to free them. In what is called the First Seminole Indian War, federal troops entered Florida to fight against the Seminole Indians and their black allies.

In early 1813, federal troops and soldiers from the Tennessee militia attacked settlements like Paynes Town in Alachua County, despite a plea from the Seminoles for peace. The federals wanted to seize Florida from the Spanish, keep out the British, and retaliate against the Seminoles, who had thwarted attempts by Americans to capture the fortress of Castillo de San Marcos in St. Augustine.

The soldiers burned down Paynes Town, took away all the food and trading items they could find, and captured hundreds of horses and cattle. The scorched-earth tactics were meant to prevent further settlement by the Seminoles there.

The campaign that General (later President) Andrew Jackson waged against the British and Seminoles in the 1810 – 1819 decade convinced the Spanish that they could not hold onto La Florida for very long.

General Andrew Jackson

13

In 1817, in a desperate attempt to regain some kind of control over La Florida, the King of Spain ceded a large tract of more than 289,000 acres as a grant to Don Fernando de la Maza Arredondo and his son for "services to the crown," provided that the land be settled by two hundred families of Spanish colonists within three years. Much of what later became the southern part of Alachua County was in that land grant.

What seemed very feasible at first, namely that Arredondo could find two hundred families to settle there, became more and more difficult as potential settlers worried about the status of Florida in terms of Indian attacks and which country would eventually control Florida: Spain or the United States.

American officials later abolished the land grants when Florida became part of the United States, but the Arredondo Grant, the land that Don Fernando was given by the Spanish Crown, would play a major role in property claims and disputes even to the present day.

Two years later, in 1819, Spain negotiated the Adams-Onís Treaty, which was signed by John Quincy Adams (U.S. Secretary of State - pictured to the left) and Luis de Onís (Spain's Minister). The agreement gave Florida to the United States and nullified the $5,000,000 debt Spain owed to the United States.

Florida now belonged to the United States.

Chapter Six: 1820 to 1829

This decade would see the admission of the territory of Florida to the United States of America, the creation of Alachua County, and the continued harassment of Native Americans.

The Adams-Onís Treaty, by which Spain ceded the territory of Florida to the United States, took effect in 1821. In the following year, the peninsula officially became a territory of the U.S. The new territory had two parts: East Florida and West Florida, two former British colonies separated by the Apalachicola River.

After the two parts were united, officials made Tallahassee the capital because the site was basically midway between the East Florida capital of St. Augustine and the West Florida capital of Pensacola. The territory's first two parts, St. Johns and Escambia, were similar to the former two parts: East and West Florida respectively.

The Santa Fe River is the boundary between Alachua and Bradford, Union, and Columbia counties.

In 1824, the Florida Legislature established Alachua County with Newnansville, located to the northeast of present-day Alachua, as its county seat. It was the ninth county of the newly acquired territory of Florida from Spain.

When the state's first railroad, which ran from Fernandina on the east coast of the state to Cedar Key on the west coast, bypassed Newnansville in favor of Gainesville in the 1850s, the latter town became the county seat.

Something happened in South Carolina in 1827 that would have a major effect on the fortunes of the Haile Family:

Colonel Benjamin Haile (1768 – 1849), whose father had originally gone from Virginia to South Carolina, discovered gold on his 1,000-acre plantation in Lancaster District in the northern part of South Carolina in the Piedmont.

An image of the creek bed where Benjamin Haile first discovered gold

He had heard that someone discovered gold in Charlotte in the Carolinas in 1827, found gold flakes in the streams on his own property the same year, and sent a shipment of the valuable ore to the U.S. Mint in Philadelphia, the first time someone had sent gold from the state.

New Gold Mine.—A letter now before us from Taxhaw, Lancaster District, dated 23d inst. states that the richest Gold Mine in the Southern States has lately been discovered in the neighborhood of that place. Seven hands from North Carolina are now employed in the mine. The prospect is highly promising, and our correspondent says, " Before long you will see our Lancaster farmers coming to market with Gold instead of Cotton,''—hope some of our subscribers live near this mine.—*Cheraw Spectator.*

*A newspaper article from 1827, shortly
after gold was discovered in the Carolinas*

As described by Louise Pettus in "Haile Gold Mine," Colonel Haile found enough of the shiny flecks to encourage him to seek out the source of the talcose slate beds above the streams.

South Carolina Gold.—We have seen more gold lately, than is quite pleasant to look at unless a man owned it himself, or had some prospect of fingering a modicum. Capt. Benjamin Haile of this town, owns a mine upon Lynch's Creek, partly in this district and partly in Lancaster, which we have no doubt, is one of the richest in the Southern States. He has already taken from it about ten thousand dollars, and the ingots which we have looked at to-day amount to something more than five thousand—the produce of only two months. Capt. Haile only works upon the surface, and that too upon a small scale. Two masses which appear evidently to have been deposited while in a state of fusion, were among the specimens exhibited to us, and are of the value of about fifty dollars.—*Camden Journal.*

A newspaper article from 1831 found in the Camden Journal

17

The historical plaque at the site of the gold mine has these words: "HAILE GOLD MINE In 1827 Benjamin Haile (1768 – 1842 [this should be 1849]) found gold here while panning in the streams on his plantation. After he found gold ore as well, Haile set up a mining operation. By 1837 the Haile Gold Mine included a 5-stamp mill, with steel stamps or pestles that crushed ore into dust from which gold was extracted. Haile leased small plots to entrepreneurs who used slave labor to mine gold.

The mine was not successful until the 1880s, when its owners hired Adolf Thies (1832 – 1917), a German mining engineer who perfected a new extraction process. A 60-stamp mill processed 100 tons a day, producing more gold than any mine east of the Mississippi. After a deadly boiler explosion in 1908, the mine closed in 1912. It operated briefly during World Wars I and II and the 1990s."

The current Haile Gold Mine's sign in front of their offices on site

A few years before discovery of gold on the plantation, Benjamin Haile's son Thomas Evans Haile was born on May 31, 1824. Thomas was the eleventh of Benjamin Haile's children, the sixth with Benjamin's second wife: Amelia White Evans.

Three years later, on May 31, 1827, the first child of Col. John Chesnut and his wife, Charlotte "Ellen" Whitaker, wealthy planters in Camden, South Carolina, was born. Her name was Esther Serena Chesnut; she would be known throughout her life as Serena.

Chapter Seven: 1830 to 1839

The election of Andrew Jackson as President of the United States in 1828 led to the passage in Congress of the Indian Removal Act in 1830 to force Indians to move west of the Mississippi River. In 1829 residents of Alachua County, Florida, wrote to President Andrew Jackson requesting federal troops for their protection from the Indians.

As pressure continued to mount on the federal government to solve the "Indian problem" in Florida, federal officials in 1832 signed the Treaty of Payne's Landing with some of the Seminole chiefs. Payne's Landing was a place on the Ocklawaha River.

The federal government promised the Indians lands west of the Mississippi River if they agreed to leave Florida voluntarily with their families. Many Seminoles left then, while those who remained prepared to defend their claims to the land. White settlers pressured the government to remove all of the Indians, by force if necessary, and in 1835, the U.S. Army arrived to enforce the treaty.

While some of the Seminole leaders agreed to be deported to the west, others did not, including Osceola, a young warrior who was one of the leaders in the Indian resistance during the Second Seminole War (1835 – 1842).

Osceola in an 1838 lithograph

19

That war, sometimes called the most expensive Indian war fought by American troops, led to the removal of many Indians to Indian Territory west of the Mississippi River, but about two or three hundred Seminoles fled south toward the Everglades. Increasing clashes between the whites and those Seminoles who remained in Florida led to the Third Seminole War (1855 – 1858). Today the descendants of those Seminoles who fled south number over twelve thousand in Florida and have done well with the opening of casinos and gaming halls.

After the Second Seminole War and the removal of many Indians, the Alachua County area enjoyed increased settlement by planters from South Carolina and Georgia. Among those settlers were children of two distinguished planters from the Camden, South Carolina area: Benjamin Haile and John Chesnut. Captain John Chesnut was the eldest son of Col. James Chesnut, a prominent planter and owner of several plantations including the famous "Mulberry Plantation," which is still standing today.

A postcard showing Mulberry Plantation

Serena Chesnut Haile's grandparents, Col. James Chesnut and Mary Cox Chesnut, built Mulberry in 1820. Serena would have spent a lot of time there as a child and young adult.

The famous diarist Mary Boykin Miller Chesnut, wife of Serena's uncle James Chesnut Jr., often stayed there and wrote in her diary. Mulberry is still owned by the family.

One member of the federal forces who fought in the Second Seminole War in Florida was John Chesnut, James Chesnut's eldest son. In early 1836, one company from South Carolina was requested by the government for a three-month tour of duty in Florida.

Colonel John Chesnut and his regiment of 76 mounted troops from the Kershaw District answered the call. Colonel Chesnut was elected Captain. John led a regiment that fought in the war and reportedly burned the villages of Negro Abraham and Micanopy (pictured to the right). One of the volunteers in that regiment was Benjamin Haile III (1810 – 1851), the son of Benjamin Haile II, the owner of the Haile Gold Mine.

When John Chesnut and Benjamin Haile III returned to South Carolina after fighting in that war, they must have praised the weather, farming conditions, and soil in Florida to their families. Some time after that, Thomas, Edward, Charles, and John Haile, younger brothers of Benjamin Haile III, as well as Thomas and James Chesnut, sons of Captain John Chesnut, moved to Florida. Captain John Chesnut, Serena Haile's father, contracted measles in Florida, a disease that developed into a very bad lung infection, and he died in 1839.

At that point, James Chesnut Jr., the remaining son of Col. James Chesnut, became the nominal head of the Chesnut Family and the heir to the Chesnut fortune.

Meanwhile, back in South Carolina, Colonel Benjamin Haile II built a facility in 1837 to process the gold he had begun to find on his property ten years before. He leased his large acreage in 50-square-foot plots to his neighbors, who used slaves to work on the gold. Some of the leased plots produced some very valuable nuggets, earning between $300 and $500 in the money of the day. Workers mined the gold down to a depth of about 25 feet, after which the operation became less profitable. The wealth generated gave more and more prestige to Colonel Haile.

After mining the gold mine for some time, Benjamin Haile's descendants leased all of the 1,900 acres to the Taylor Brothers of Charlotte for $20,000 in Confederate money. Those who leased the land agreed to give much of the gold and other minerals to help the Confederacy in the war effort.

A sample of Confederate money

Chapter Eight: 1840 to 1849

This decade was an important one for the territory of Florida and for the Hailes' move south to that territory. In 1842, the Second Seminole War ended after seven long years of fighting. Historians have called that war the longest, bloodiest, and most expensive Indian war in the history of our nation.

Although there would be more clashes with Native Americans and, in fact, another war with the Seminoles, the relative quiet in the northern part of the territory allowed more white settlers to move into that part, settle down with their families, and raise crops and cattle.

Much of that was helped along when the U.S. Congress passed in 1842 the Armed Occupation Act, which provided free land to settlers who improved the land and promised to fight the Indians if necessary.

In 1845, Florida entered the Union as the 27th state, a slave state. As was the practice in those days, in order to keep a balance of slave and free states in the U.S. Senate, Iowa was admitted the next year as a free state. In 1845, Florida had only around seventy thousand residents, many of whom were slaves.

Later during the War between the States some freed slaves joined the Union Army.

This decade was also a busy one for the Hailes in South Carolina. Esther Serena Chesnut, who attended Miss Hawks School in Philadelphia, Pennsylvania (1843 – 1844), married Thomas Evans Haile on March 13, 1847, at the home of Serena's mother: Charlotte Ellen Whitaker Chesnut in Camden, South Carolina. Serena gave birth to two children that decade: John Chesnut Haile on January 14, 1848, in Camden; Ellen Whitaker Haile on March 28, 1849, also in Camden.

Colonel Benjamin Haile II, the patriarch of the family who had brought the family much wealth from the gold he discovered on his South Carolina property, had two wives. His first wife was Mary Cureton Haile, with whom he had five children: James Cureton, Benjamin III, Catherine (who would marry Christopher Matheson), Susan, and Sarah.

Benjamin Haile II's second wife was Amelia White Evans Haile (1795 – 1880). Her father was Charles Evans, a "man of property, noted for his livestock"; he was an ardent patriot during the Revolution, was captured by the British and Tories, and was taken to Charleston. Amelia's mother was Mary W. Blakeney, who died in 1857.

A piano on display at the house today

24

Benjamin Haile II and Amelia had ten children: Mary, Caroline, Rebecca, Columbus, Elizabeth, Thomas Evans, Edward, William, John, and Charles Evans. Amelia owned the Duncan Phyfe sofa which is now in the Homestead's parlor (see image of the sofa on p. 111). Amelia is buried in the Kanapaha Church Cemetery. For more about the genealogy of the Haile Family, see Appendix A.

On June 26, 1849, Colonel Benjamin Haile II, the patriarch of the family who had brought the family much wealth from the gold he discovered on his South Carolina property, died in Camden at the age of 81 and was buried in the Old Quaker Cemetery there.

When Benjamin Haile II died in 1849, he left most of his estate to his older sons. Thomas Haile inherited 1,500 acres, enslaved laborers, and $4,000, a considerable fortune at that time.

Benjamin Haile II's house in Camden

Unfortunately, four consecutive bad cotton crops at their Little Lynches Creek plantation discouraged the younger Hailes.

Two views of a house of Benjamin Haile II's son, James C. Haile

Chapter Nine: 1850 to 1859

The decade of the 1850s brought more stability to the State of Florida as more and more Native Americans were shipped west, and then many settlers arrived here in search of good land on which they could grow crops. Alachua County attracted many new residents because of its beauty (several lakes with good fishing, temperate climate), possibilities (large tracts of land on which to grow crops like oranges and cotton and also raise cattle), and the potential (access to northern markets by road and eventually by train).

The brands of Spanish cattle in Florida

Cattle ranchers in Alachua County did well, following the lead of the Spanish who had raised cattle here when they controlled Florida in the seventeenth century. In terms of which crops to grow, some farmers, like the Hailes, chose cotton, although those farmers in the rich so-called Middle Florida area, for example around Tallahassee, would do better because of the conditions there.

Some farmers raised oranges, a practice which also harkened back to the earlier Spaniards and Catholic missionaries (who had planted seeds in the seventeenth century) or Native Americans (who had become fond of citrus). What would eventually end the harvesting of oranges here were devastating freezes in the 1890s.

27

Meanwhile up in South Carolina, the 1850s would bring a major move for the Hailes as they packed up their goods and made the long trip to Florida, where they would begin their lives anew. Four crop failures forced the Hailes to make the difficult decision to move.

Haile family tradition says that Thomas's older brother made note of the fertile soil he found in Florida when he was here in 1836 to fight in the Second Seminole War. He thought it would be good soil for growing Sea Island Cotton, which was their cash crop in South Carolina.

The 1850 census for Kershaw County, South Carolina, listed Thos. E. Haile, age 26, farmer, real estate valued at $20,000; his wife, Serena Haile, age 23, his wife; John C. Haile, age 3; and Ellen W. Haile, age 1.

This is the only known picture of Thomas and Serena Haile's house in Camden - in 1854, when they moved to Florida.

Thomas and Serena Haile and their four children (one child, a daughter, had died as a toddler) left Camden, South Carolina, on March 17, 1854, for Florida after four successive crop failures due to flooding. The family traveled to Charleston and then by boat to Florida. They also had with them an unspecified number of enslaved laborers.

The toddler who died, Ellen Whitaker Haile (March 28, 1849 - July 27, 1850, the second child of Thomas and Serena, is buried in the Old Quaker Cemetery in Camden, South Carolina.

The grave marker of Ellen Whitaker Haile in the Old Quaker Cemetery

The Hailes planted their first cotton crops here in March 1855, plowing around trees to do so. It was a successful crop. They also planted rice. Land was very cheap too - Thomas having paid $1/acre for some of the land. The tax rolls of 1854 show the Hailes in Florida with 56 enslaved people.

The family's choice of a place to settle down, the present Haile Homestead land, was a good one. When plans were being made to construct the state's first cross-state railroad from Fernandina on the northeast corner of Florida to Cedar Key on the Gulf of Mexico, local officials in 1853 decided to move the county seat from Newnansville, which was near the present-day town of Alachua, to Gainesville in order to be much closer to the railroad, which would be finished in 1860 (see next chapter).

The new railroad would be on the southern edge of the Haile Homestead property where Archer Road (S.R. 24) is today.

The Hailes bought approximately 1,500 acres of the Arredondo Grant from Henry Marquand, Richard Miller, and others. That grant was from the Spanish king in 1817, at a time when Spain nominally controlled Florida, to a Spanish merchant, Don Fernando de la Maza Arredondo, in hopes that he would settle what became Alachua County (see Chapter Five). The total land mass in that grant was a little less than 300,000 acres. Thomas Haile named his 1,500-acre plantation Kanapaha after the area he settled in.

The fenced-off cistern on the property today

Apparently, Thomas and Serena Haile lived with their children in a small log house near Fort Clarke while they had enslaved craftsmen construct their new home. Thomas's brother Edward and Serena's brother, Thomas W. Chesnut, purchased property in the area as well. Their first cotton crop at their new residence did so well that they convinced other family members to move to Alachua County in the following years. Ultimately, there would be three of Thomas's brothers (Edward, Charles, and John), their mother (Amelia), and two of Serena's brothers (James and Thomas Chesnut) living in Alachua County.

Kanapaha Presbyterian Church

What follows is a description of the church they helped establish and the magnificent home they built, a home that still survives today on its original site - with some restoration - in remarkable condition. The information comes from oral histories of family members and surveys by architects. Thomas and Serena Haile, who were invited by an uncle to join him in Missouri, went to Charleston, South Carolina, with the intention of booking passage on a ship to Norfolk, Virginia, and then overland to Missouri. However, once in Charleston, they found that they could not book passage to Norfolk, but could book passage to Florida, which they did.

Once in Florida, they bought approximately 1,500 acres of land at $1 to $1.25/acre and settled down. After a successful crop of Sea Island Cotton, they and their like-minded neighbors thought about establishing a Presbyterian church here. In 1857, they called a meeting of their neighbors, among whom were Thomas Chesnut, Ely Ramsey, Dr. W.H. Stringfellow, Dr. Robert Stuart, John D. Young, and others.

The Hailes and some of their neighbors commissioned Dr. Stringfellow to return to South Carolina and convince their former pastor there, the Rev. William J. McCormick and his family, to come to Florida and help establish a church here. Much of the information here is from *Planters, Plantations & Presbyterians: Kanapaha & Reverend W.J. McCormick* by F.D. McCormick.

31

Rev. McCormick preached his first sermon in Florida in January 1858, then moved down with his wife and three young daughters to begin their new life here in January 1859. Rev. McCormick held services at the Fort Clarke Church on the plantation of Dr. Stringfellow while the Kanapaha Presbyterian Church was being built.

In April 1859, the first Kanapaha Church was finished, and the church was formally organized with twelve members and two elders: Dr. W.H. Stringfellow and Joseph A. Scott. In November 1859, the church was united with the Presbytery of Florida at Jacksonville. The first building's dimensions resembled those of subsequent structures. (See image of the modern building on the previous page.)

During the War between the States the church fell into a state of disrepair. In 1886 the congregation built a new church building a little further to the west near the new train depot called South Arredondo. The following year the stop was renamed Kanapaha. The historic 1886 Kanapaha Presbyterian Church still stands today, with many of its original features, at 6221 S.W. 75th Terrace.

The church cemetery sign – the white arrow points to the Haile plot, where members of the Haile Family have been buried.

The Kanapaha Presbyterian Church Cemetery was established around the church after its construction in 1859. The earliest marked burial belongs to John Chesnut Haile, Thomas and Serena Haile's eldest child, who died in 1867.

In the oldest-known photo of the original church (see next page), the gates of the Haile family enclosure (with the oldest dated grave - 1867) can be seen.

It is located today at 4101 S.W. 63rd Boulevard, which is 1.7 miles west of I-75. The cemetery is .7 miles down S.W. 63rd Boulevard on the right-hand side. The Haile Homestead is another 1.7 miles west of S.W. 63rd Boulevard.

The gate to the Haile Family plot in the Kanapaha Cemetery

Moses Ramsey donated land at Arredondo, along the old military road which connected Ft. Clarke with the forts in Micanopy and Newnansville. In April 1859, the construction of the church was completed and the congregation was formally organized.

Reverend McCormick went on to organize Presbyterian churches in Micanopy, Archer, Fort King, and Wacahoota. Interestingly, Kanapaha Presbyterian Church was the mother church of First Presbyterian Church in Gainesville, which was organized in March 1867.

This very old picture, which was recently acquired
from Evans Haile, has on the back a note saying
that the church was in the middle of the cemetery.
It is possible for one to see the gate
to the Haile enclosure to the right of the horse.
Lake Kanapaha was east of the church.
(See the previous page for a photo of the cemetery gate today.)

The Homestead

The Haile Homestead has today the following structures: the main house, a fenced-off cistern, the chimney from the caretaker's house, and the remains of a collapsed cabin in the northeast corner of the property. The house never had indoor plumbing, although remnants of the outhouse have not been found. The house has no remnants of the kitchen other than stones used at the corners and in the hearth, but the house used to have a detached kitchen which burned down in the 1920s. It was in the backyard to the northeast. Changes to the manse over the subsequent years include the removal and replacement of a chimney, replacement of the original cypress shake roof with a metal one in the 1930s, a cedar one in the 1990s and the current pine shake roof in 2013, and the replacement of the front columns. Electricity was discreetly added for the making of the movie "Gal Young 'Un" in the 1970s.

Workers built the main house over two sturdy tree trunks, which one can still see under the house. Henry Gaines, the enslaved stone mason from the Dr. W.H. Stringfellow plantation up at Fort Clarke, built the limestone piers under the house. The house was reportedly built on piers for ventilation purposes. The mortared lime-rock piers under the house stand almost four feet tall. Workers primarily used the strong heart of pine for the beams, running the entire length of the front porch. The marks left by their axes are still visible today.

Strong pillars under the house support it well.

35

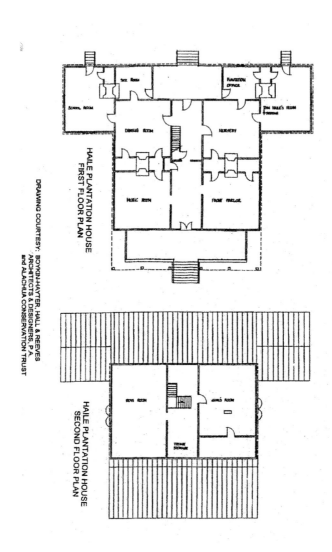

A layout of the house

The house, which is a story-and-a-half tall, has about 6,200 square feet under roof. It has ten rooms and two center halls (see layout of the house on the previous page).

The Hailes used one downstairs room as a schoolroom for their own children and the children of their neighbors, while they used another such room as a nursery for the youngest children.

The music room
toward the front of the house

The two upstairs rooms consisted of a boys' dormitory and a girls' dormitory for the twelve boys and two girls in the family, although probably no more than ten boys occupied the one room at the same time, because one son (John) died in 1867, and another (Carol) wasn't born until 1870.

The roof covers the front porch and rests on six solid square tapered wood pillars over limestone bases beyond the porch. This architectural feature is known as a rain porch and can be found on many antebellum homes in the Camden area. The roof originally had cypress shingles, but workers replaced them in 1937 with standing seam galvanized metal and again with cedar shingles in the 1990s' restoration. In 2013 a pine shake roof was put on. The house has both hand-hewn and sawed boards, which indicates that a saw mill provided at least part of the lumber during the construction, which lasted almost two years.

The house is braced frame construction with the framing members spaced from 25 to 30 inches on center. Workers pegged the larger vertical studs into the floor girders. Those workers mortised the secondary members into the girders and used cut nails throughout the house. The siding has vertical corner boards on the north and south walls.

Twelve-foot ceilings and large windows with louvered shutters helped the family cope with Florida's heat, while four brick chimneys and eight fireplaces on the first floor provided warmth in the winter. Although the interior trim is very simple, the hardware was molded cast iron "Cottage" pattern with mottled brown porcelain Rockingham knobs, imported from the North. The shutters were held back with wrought-iron fixtures.

The double-door main entry (see picture above) is flanked by glass sidelights and a transom. The doors are two-paneled throughout the house and the walls are finished with ¾ to 1 inch thick horsehair plaster over lath. The plaster walls were originally painted white, but now have writing on them, i.e. are what are called "Talking Walls." The scale and excellent construction attest to the skill of the enslaved craftsmen who built the house.

38

Photos of the different rooms at the Haile Homestead

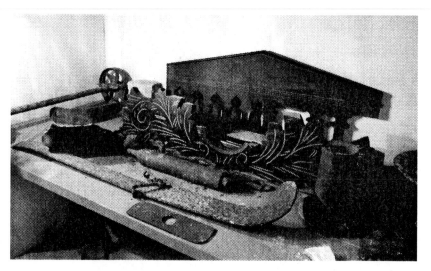

Artifacts found at the house during restoration

An original crib in the nursery
The crib was repaired and restored by Back in Time Restoration.

*A wardrobe with a dress inside that
belonged to Maud Graham Haile*

This is an incubator for chicken eggs.
It would have been in one of the three barns out back.

The icebox is a relic of the party days, circa 1900.

This bed is an original one in the Girls' Room upstairs.

This bed is one of two homemade beds in the Boys' Room.
One has Roman numerals etched into the side rail where the slats go.

This trunk was from Maud Graham Haile's family.

The marble-top table is believed to be original.

Chapter Ten: 1860 to 1869

The 1860s were a very difficult time in the South, including Florida, when the War between the States tore apart families and the lifestyle that generations of white planters had enjoyed.

The first railroad to connect both Florida coasts, joining Fernandina on the Atlantic and Cedar Key on the Gulf, was completed in 1860. From Gainesville it headed to Cedar Key along what today is S.R. 24. The railroad was to greatly help the towns along the line and allow farmers like the Hailes to ship their goods to cities in different parts of the country. At least, that was the plan.

The Financial Panic of 1857 drove the railroad to the edge of bankruptcy, and its owner, U.S. Senator David Levy Yulee, lost control of it. The whole line stretched 156 miles, making it the longest railroad finished before the War between the States.

The restored original train station in Fernandina on Florida's first cross-state railroad

When the 1860 census was taken, the Hailes as a group were the largest slaveholders in Alachua County. Amelia Haile had 174 enslaved laborers on her plantation, Edward Haile had 101, Thomas Haile had 66, and John Haile had 59, as did Thomas Chesnut.

Meanwhile, Florida's cross-state railroad was about to suffer a disaster, just as it began running in the early 1860s. A Union gunboat raided Cedar Key in January 1862 and destroyed many of the railroad's buildings. Another gunboat attacked Fernandina in March of that year and did much damage to the last train leaving the town, killing or injuring several passengers. The owner of the line, Senator Yulee, almost lost his life in the incident.

Senator David Levy Yulee

In the next two years, troops from both sides of the war pulled up the iron rails for use elsewhere. The line later became part of the Seaboard Air Line Railroad and, where it still operates, is run by CSX Transportation and the First Coast Railroad.

In 1861, war came to the South. The Hailes, like most of the transplanted South Carolinians, were staunch Confederates. Thomas Haile and his teenage oldest son, John, enlisted in the Fifth Battalion Cavalry in 1863. Thomas became a lieutenant who participated with Col. J. J. Dickison's Second Florida Cavalry in February 1865 in a raid on Braddock's Farm just south of Crescent City.

In December 1862 Serena's youngest sister Ellen died at the Homestead, according to her obituary. It is unknown whether she was visiting the Hailes or had moved there with them. Her body was transported back to Camden and buried in the Knights Hill cemetery.

Back in South Carolina, Union General William Tecumseh Sherman (1820 – 1891) had his troops destroy the equipment at the Haile Gold Mine. The Haile family lost control of the land to James Ethridge, a man from New York who owned the Hobkirk Inn in Camden, South Carolina.

A new process succeeded in extracting gold from the low-grade ore found in the mine. Workers were able to extract as many as one hundred tons of ore a day from the mine. The mine continued to produce gold until an explosion in 1908 destroyed much of the equipment and killed three workers. The owners closed the mine in 1912 after a record number of years of producing gold, longer and more successfully than any other mine in the eastern United States. The mine was eventually purchased by Romarco Minerals Inc. and in 2011 was confirmed to have more than 2 million ounces in gold reserves. (Haile Gold Mine website: www.hailegoldmine.com)

There has been much speculation about the Confederate gold that disappeared after Jefferson Davis (pictured here to the right) was captured at the end of the war.

At the end of the war, the Haile Homestead provided shelter to members of the Confederate baggage and treasure train during its 1865 flight to David Yulee's Cottonwood Plantation in Archer, Florida. After the party reached its destination and learned of Jefferson Davis's capture in Georgia, the remainder of the treasury was allegedly divided up, and the members of the party dispersed. Two members of the treasure train's escort, Tench Francis Tilghman and Sid Winder, stayed one night at the Homestead on May 24th on their way out of town.

The question of enslaved laborers is an important one in the discussion about the building and maintaining of the Haile Homestead. While we cannot be sure about the exact number of enslaved laborers who accompanied the Hailes from South Carolina to their new home in Alachua County, the 1860 census listed 66 enslaved people dwelling in 18 cabins on the Kanapaha Plantation.

The tax roll for the same year, however, listed 79 enslaved people. Researchers have learned much by interviewing the descendants of Ned Chisholm, a man enslaved on the Stringfellow Plantation in the Fort Clarke area to the north of Kanapaha. Ned Chisholm may have been lent to the Hailes for the building of the Homestead, especially for putting on the roof.

Another enslaved craftsman from the Stringfellow Plantation, Henry Gaines, a stonemason, may have built the limestone piers under the house, as well as the chimneys and the fireplaces. Embedded in the base of the nursery room's fireplace is what appears to be a flat iron and an andiron, possibly left by Henry Gaines as a good luck charm (pictured to the right).

Other enslaved carpenters who were living at Kanapaha were Johnson Chestnut and William "Uncle Billy" Watts. Johnson Chestnut, a skilled furniture maker, made some of the pieces of furniture on display at the Homestead. His descendants are very active in local politics and in the business community. Oral tradition says that Johnson put a "t" in the middle of "Chesnut" to differentiate the black from the white Chesnuts.

In the extant portion of Serena Haile's journal, she refers to many "hands" she employed, people who presumably were once slaves. It is clear from her writing that Bennet Kelley held a special place in her heart. Beginning in 1883, she mentions Bennet almost daily. Bennet, the son of Edmund and Charity Kelley, both enslaved at Kanapaha, was born in 1844, according to his grave marker.

The grave marker of Bennet(t) Kelley in the Kanapaha Cemetery has "Bennett," but the family consistently spelled it "Bennet."

Later census data shows his birth year as 1849. Family tradition says that Bennet was the houseboy, and as such would have worked in the Homestead and been close to the family. No record of Bennet's whereabouts during almost two decades following the War between the States has been found other than his appearance on the 1870 census showing his parents and siblings still living on or near Kanapaha. We do know that Bennet married Mary Hodison in 1876. From the time his name first appears in the journal in 1883, it is clear that he is more than a field hand. He performs many household chores and even makes Serena breakfast after the cook quits. In December 1884 Serena notes that a cabin from "the yard" was torn down and reassembled behind the house for Bennet.

According to the journal, Mary died of the "grippe" or flu in February 1892. Bennet was remarried a few months later to a woman named Daphne. Unfortunately her last name is illegible in the journal. The marriage license in Alachua County's ancient records lists her last name as Summers, but the oral history of descendants of enslaved laborers says that she was a DeBose. In fact, her 1933 death certificate shows that her father's name was Joe DeBose.

Haile family tradition holds that Bennet was so close to the family that Serena Haile left instructions that Bennet should be buried in the family plot in the Kanapaha Presbyterian Church Cemetery (see a photo on the previous page of Bennet's grave marker). Although Bennet died in 1933, many years after Serena Haile's death in 1895, the family honored her request and buried him in a corner of the family plot. Pictures of Bennet and his wife are on display at the Homestead.

All that is left of the house that Bennet lived in behind the main house is this dilapidated chimney.

Research continues into the identity and lives of the enslaved workers at Kanapaha Plantation. While Alachua County maintained relatively good records in the 1800s, many of which have been imaged and are available through the Clerk of the Court's Ancient Records website, we are dependent upon oral histories of descendants to fill in some of the blanks. Like any story passed from one person to the next, especially through the years, there are bound to be inaccuracies and details which can never be verified.

So far, however, the written records that have been found seem to support much of what has been passed down through time. The importance of the contribution of enslaved laborers to the survival and success of planters throughout the South cannot be emphasized enough. The fact that the Homestead is still standing today is a testament to the skills and abilities of the enslaved people who built it. Many of their stories remain to be told.

Pictured to the left is the only known photograph of John Chesnut Haile (1848 - 1867), Thomas and Serena's eldest child. He rode with his father in the Fifth Cavalry Battalion CSA. He died at the age of 19 and is the earliest dated burial in the Kanapaha Presbyterian Church Cemetery. The pain of losing her first child is evident in Serena's diary as, many years later in the 1880s, she remembers his birthday or the anniversary of his death.

The Hailes continued to grow cotton at the end of the war due to high demand. After the war ended, some of Thomas's freed slaves chose to remain as tenant farmers. A mortgage record dated May 15, 1873 shows Thomas Haile with five tenant farmers, among them Edward (Edmund) Kelley and William Watts, both of whom had been enslaved at Kanapaha. Brother Edward Haile opened a mercantile business, Savage & Haile, in Gainesville. His success may have been due to his acceptance of crops and mortgages in lieu of cash.

The Haile family did pretty well in those difficult years after the war until their cotton crop failed in 1867, a failure brought on by much rain that year. By that year (1867), Thomas Haile was experiencing serious financial problems. In addition to the death of his eldest son, John, who died that year shortly after his 19th birthday, the Hailes experienced a crop failure due to a combination of heavy rains and caterpillars.

The shaded front porch has seen many, many visitors.

At some point after the war, Thomas Haile returned to Camden to recruit freedmen to come to Florida to work on his plantation. It is unknown whether or not he met with success.

Also in 1867 Ned Chisholm, the enslaved craftsman who put the roof on the Hailes' house, went together with his two brothers and purchased two full sections of land (1,280 acres) on the west side of Newnan's Lake, paying for it with 35,000 pounds of Sea Island Cotton. Although the crop failed that year, they were given an extension of time to pay.

In 1866, after the war, officials combined the Gainesville Academy, which was the town's first school, with Ocala's East Florida Seminary (see Chapter Twelve for more about this).

In 1867 land was acquired for the building of Union Academy for the education of freedmen. Johnson Chestnut, who had been an enslaved furniture maker at Kanapaha, was among the trustees of the school. (ref. Deed Book G pg 522-523)

*Union Academy opened in Gainesville soon after the close
of the Civil War. Federal officials had the school built,
partly with funds from contributors in the North
and partly with funds from the George Peabody Fund.*

On April 14, 1869, town officials incorporated Gainesville.

Alachua County's first courthouse in Gainesville, built in 1856 at a cost of $5000, would be torn down in 1884 when a new courthouse was built. The county seat had been at Newnansville, but was moved to Gainesville in 1853.

In 1868, Thomas Haile declared bankruptcy, and his plantation was put up for auction. His brother Edward purchased the property (1,800 acres in all) for $720 on September 16, 1868 (Deed record G page 736-737). His brother Edward was able to provide the necessary funds to keep the property in the family. The Hailes continued to acquire property after that, until they amassed about as much land as they had before the bankruptcy.

On June 11, 1869, Evans Haile, the fourteenth child of Thomas Evans and Serena Haile, was born at the Kanapaha Plantation. He would live for sixty-five years, finally dying in 1934 after a long successful life as a husband, father, and attorney. Evans married Maud Graham on April 18, 1906, in Gainesville, and they had two children: James Graham Haile and Thomas Evans Haile.

Chapter Eleven: 1870 to 1879

On December 15, 1870, Thomas and Serena Haile com-
pleted their family with the birth of their fifteenth and last child, a

boy named Carol Matheson Haile
(pictured here). Serena was 43 at
the time of his birth.

Carol was employed by the
railroad and frequently stopped
by the Homestead between runs.
By 1893 he was living in Baldwin, Florida, where he married
Henrietta (Etta) Dupray (1878 –
1965) on March 7, 1894. Their
first child, Louise Dupray Haile
was born in 1895 at Baldwin.
The family moved to Jacksonville
where son Elwood Evans Haile was born and died (1896-1897).
At the time of his father's death in 1896, Carol was a trace clerk of
the Southern Express Company.

In July of 1900 Carol and Etta welcomed daughter Caro-
lyn. The census shows Carol as a clerk living at 330 First Street in
Jacksonville. In April 1906 twins came along: Mildred Love Haile
and Walter Kennedy Haile. By 1910 Carol was a railroad auditor
living at 1731 Hubbard Street. He was general agent with the Seaboard Air Line Railroad Company before becoming general Florida agent with the Merchants and Miners Steamship Company.

He was a deacon and trustee of the Springfield Presbyterian Church, a charter member of the Traffic Club, and long standing member of the Jacksonville Kiwanis Club. The family was
living at 2616 Hubbard Street, Jacksonville, when Carol died on
August 18, 1955. Carol and Etta are buried beside each other in
Evergreen Cemetery, Jacksonville, Florida.

A granddaughter of Carol and Etta Haile, Henrietta Vinson of Virginia, shared many fond memories of her grandfather. Carol told her how he remembered sitting on the floor of the old Homestead looking up at the crystal chandelier, which is long gone, hanging from the ceiling.

He shared with her his great pride at being the first person to ring the bell of the "new" Kanapaha Presbyterian Church in 1886 when he was just 16 years old.

Carol had a special place in his heart for Bennet Kelley, with whom he spent many hours as a young boy at the Homestead. Bennet, a former slave of the Hailes still living behind the old Homestead in the 1920s, made a special trip to Jacksonville to visit Carol. Unfortunately Bennet experienced the effects of Jim Crow laws when he was forced to urinate behind a sign somewhere. That experience left its mark on Bennet, who, by that time, was a very old man. He said he'd never return to Jacksonville. And he also preferred the quiet of the country to the loud noises and commotion in a big city. (The men are pictured to the left.)

Mrs. Vinson shared her grandfather's recollection of one of Bennet's common expressions: "Do Jesus!" As in "Do Jesus – I just seen a snake!" Henrietta said her grandfather visited the Homestead many times after his move to Jacksonville because he loved the place so much.

Etta   and   Carol Haile

In 1872, Amelia E. "Millie" Haile, the Hailes' eldest daughter, married Robert Fenwick Taylor, and they had three children: Carl Hugo, Serena Haile, and an unnamed baby girl who died as an infant.

Amelia's husband went by the name of Fenwick, but was called "Fen" by the family and sometimes as "Mr. T." in Serena's diary.

He lived a relatively long life (1849-1928), was a Florida lawyer and Democratic politician, and served on the Florida Supreme Court (1891-1925) and as Chief Justice for three terms (1897-1905, 1915-1917, and 1923-1925).

Robert Fenwick Taylor (pictured to the right) was born in Myrtle Hill, South Carolina, and was tutored at home in Marion County, Florida, where his family moved before he was three.

Taylor fought as a volunteer in the Battle of Gainesville (1864) during the War Between the States.

After the war, he attended Baltimore's Maryland Military Institute before returning to Gainesville to study law with his brother-in-law, attorney James B. Dawkins, a member of the Congress of the Confederate States.

In 1870, Taylor was admitted to the Ocala Bar, practiced law in Gainesville, and later attended the constitutional convention of 1885. He was appointed to the Florida Supreme Court in 1891 by Governor Francis Fleming to replace an outgoing Justice.

He was reelected six times to the Court, where he heard more than seven thousand cases and wrote more than five hundred opinions. He was particularly known as a conservative defender of personal and property rights.

Taylor died of pneumonia and kidney failure in 1928 at his home in Tallahassee. (See Chapter Fourteen for more details about that family.)

*Above is a picture of the Haile children (l-r) taken in the 1870s:
George Reynolds Haile (1865-1934), Mary Chesnut Haile
(later Budd) (1859-1938), and Sydney Haile (1864-1938).*

The Hailes learned an important lesson from the failure of
their Sea Island cotton crops in 1867. They diversified their plant-
ings, growing oranges, Peento peaches, Kelsey plums, cantaloupe,
watermelon, squash, Irish potatoes, sweet potatoes, pinders, etc.,
enough to sustain their family as well as to sell.

In December 1873, the Hailes had recovered enough finan-
cially to purchase the title to their house and forty acres around it
from Edward Haile for $500. They also purchased another 70-acre
piece from Edward for $100. Serena Haile alone is listed as the
grantee on both deeds (Deed Record I pages 143-145).

The Haile family plot in the Kanapaha Presbyterian Church Cemetery

The picture above was taken at the Homestead while the family was still growing oranges. This would have been in the 1870s - 1890s.

Chapter Twelve: 1880 to 1889

Although David Yulee's railroad from Fernandina on the east coast to Cedar Key on the west coast was destroyed by both sides during the War between the States, after the war developers built rail lines throughout the state, which greatly facilitated the shipment of goods to and from Florida.

During that war, the Kanapaha Presbyterian Church that the Hailes had helped build fell into disrepair, and the congregation worshipped at several local plantations. In 1885, when local residents learned that a new train depot was to be built to the west of Arredondo, to be called South Arredondo, the congregation saw an opportunity to rebuild their church.

One person who died that decade was Amelia Evans Haile (1795 - 1880), mother of Thomas Haile and his brothers. She is pictured to the left. She was also the wife of gold mine owner Benjamin Haile II. She was said to be a generous woman, having donated half the funds (along with Mrs. Sarah Ciples) to build the parsonage for the Lyttleton Street Methodist Church in Camden, South Carolina (see photo on the next page).

She moved to Alachua County with her sons in the 1850s and had a plantation in the Jonesville area. She has the earliest birthdate of all the marked graves in the Kanapaha Presbyterian Church Cemetery.

*A recent photo of the Lyttleton Street Methodist Church parsonage,
which Amelia Haile helped pay for; the parsonage is now
on Greene Street in Camden, South Carolina.*

Another Haile who died that decade was one of the sons, Thomas Evans Haile Jr. (1853 - 1885) - pictured to the left. He died unmarried at the Homestead.

Serena gave a detailed account of his death on December 29, 1885 in the diary: "Tues 29th Dr. McK here, Tom dying – Oh such suffering in morning – Died at 5 P.M Tuesday Dec. 29th – passed away peacefully & calmly – thank God.

62

Oh the anguish of this time – All that could be done was done – Oh my child, my child --Wed 30th Cold – Clear Many friends with us - We laid him to rest beside his brother John, in Churchyard just at twilight – Dec 30th. Such sympathy & respect from all –

Thurs 31st Oh how little I thought that this last day of year I & all would be in such sorrow –"

Today his grave marker bears 1886 as his year of death. At some point his original marker was stolen or destroyed and a family Bible used to obtain the dates. Unfortunately, a sibling recorded his year of death incorrectly, leading to the error on his marker.

Mary Chesnut Haile, the Hailes' youngest surviving daughter, married Josiah T. Budd II of Monticello, Fl in March 1881 - with Rev. William J. McCormick officiating.

*Photos of Mary Chesnut Haile Budd and Josiah T. Budd II
taken during their honeymoon in March 1881*

63

Serena's diary entry for March 24, 1881 says: "Thursday 24th Mary Haile & Mr Budd married – 8 o'clock A.M Left on Train."

Mary, the ninth child of Thomas Evans and Serena Haile, was born at Kanapaha in 1859. She died in 1938 in Quincy, Florida and is buried in Roseland Cemetery in Monticello. Josiah Budd II (1855 – 1930) was a prominent merchant in Monticello. Together Mary and Josiah would have five children: Katie, Elizabeth "Lizzie," Josephine "Josie," Amelia "Millie" (who died as a toddler), and Josiah T. Budd III. Serena recorded the heights of some of the young Budds on the wall of the Master Bedroom.

A picture of the furniture in the parlor that Mary and Josiah T. Budd purchased in 1882 - one of Mary's granddaughters, Miss Mary Budd Holmes of Monticello, Florida, donated the furniture to the house. She is the daughter of Mary and Josiah's daughter, Katie A. Budd.

In August 1885, the congregation of Kanapaha Church appointed a committee to see about building a new church near the site of the new railroad depot.

*The very rare photo to the left
shows the church
with its original 1886 pointed steeple.*

On June 26, 1886, members of the church laid the cornerstone of the new church. They completed the building of the new church by September 1886. That church building still remains today at that site: 6221 SW 75th Terrace, and has an active, vibrant congregation. (See www.kanapaha.net)

The image to the right shows the steeple after a stubbier version of the original was installed after hurricanes in the 1940s destroyed the original one.

A year later in 1887, the train depot was renamed Kanapaha. Reverend McCormick, the pastor who had moved from South Carolina to minister to the congregation, passed away of typhoid pneumonia on June 29, 1883. He was never to see this new church building.

65

Until 1886, the closest major stop for the Hailes was in Arredondo, where the old military or stage road crossed and near where the original Kanapaha Presbyterian Church was built.

There were stores as well. In 1886, a new depot just to the west was opened and called "South Arredondo." A year later in 1887, it was renamed "Kanapaha."

Because Serena Haile's diary from this period survived, many of the details about the construction of the church were preserved. For instance, the young men of the congregation spent a whole day installing the kerosene chandelier on November 12, 1886.

The red bordered stained glass windows along both sides of the sanctuary and the back of the sanctuary were purchased with money raised by Serena Haile and other women of the church by selling ice cream from the back of their wagons.

To the right is a picture of the Hailes' daughter, Mary Chesnut Haile Budd, along with Alexina Jessie Chesnut Gibbes Holmes (Mary's cousin and the daughter of Serena's brother, Thomas W. Chesnut and Helen Taylor Chesnut).

Services were held twice on Sundays, with a prayer meeting on Wednesdays. The Hailes' youngest child, sixteen-year-old Carol Matheson Haile, was proud to have been the first person to ring the new bell.

Serena Haile noted in her diary that she could hear it ringing from her porch. It was made by Henry McShane & Co. of Baltimore, Maryland and arrived on October 14, 1886. It was installed by the men of the congregation on November 11th of the same year.

Today these historical features remain, including the original pews. The kerosene chandelier illuminates the sanctuary only once a year, on Christmas Eve. The original steeple, badly damaged by hurricanes in the 1940s, was restored in 2001.

The interior of the Kanapaha Presbyterian Church
showing the original kerosene chandelier,
red-bordered stained-glass windows, and pews

A few of the Hailes' sons either worked for the railroad (such as Walter) or held jobs associated with the railroad, for example with the Messenger Service or as a freight clerk (Carol). Serena would go down to one of the depots and chat with her sons as they passed through when the trains stopped. She also reported various train accidents and such.

In reading Serena Haile's diary/journal, we can learn much about life at the Homestead and in the surrounding area. For example, concerning the local Presbyterian church that she and her husband helped found: "Fri Nov 7th [1884] Clear & bright morn - Cold - Clouded up around 11 am - Drizzly all day - raw & uncomfortable - George & Bennet went to Churchyard to sweep out church."

Another entry from Mrs. Haile's journal logs the following: "Sunday Nov 9th [1884] a cloudy raw day - 'Mr Baker' here - Preached at Kanapaha Church - A Good Sermon - every body liked him - a large Congregation. Meeting for subscription for Minister's salary. Mr Baker staid the night - with us - Preached 4 pm at School house"

Serena Haile's Journal 1874 -1893

Based on the accounts in Serena's diary, it appears that the original Kanapaha church remained in use at least until the beginning of 1885 and was probably deliberately dismantled and its materials salvaged for the building of the new structure further west.

68

In Serena's diary on January 10, 1885, she noted that Mr. Curry preached at Kanapaha Church. But on January 21st Mr. Hough conducted the "first prayer meeting" in the "Schoolhouse." On Sunday June 29th she noted that preaching was done at the Schoolhouse.

Serena's last reference to "Kanapaha Church" (vs. the Schoolhouse) was on Easter Sunday, April 5, 1885, where she noted the church was decorated prettily. From that point on, she refers to the Schoolhouse or simply uses the term "church" non-specifically. One could assume that the old Kanapaha Church was no longer in use some time after Easter in April 1885.

On June 28, 1885, the Hailes' grandson Carl Hugo Taylor (b. 1882), the son of Millie and Fen Taylor, was christened at the Schoolhouse by Mr. Hough. For an event as important as the christening of their first grandson, one can be reasonably sure the old church was no longer available for use, else the Hailes would have had him christened there. Serena's diary also dispels old lore that the old church burned down. Had such a fire occurred, it would have been big news in her diary.

The grave site in the Kanapaha Presbyterian Church Cemetery of Amelia Evans Haile (1795 - 1880), mother of Thomas Haile and his brothers, as well as the wife of gold mine owner Benjamin Haile II.

E v a n s Haile (pictured to the right) attended East Florida Seminary (EFS). He is proudly wearing two medals he won: in 1887 he won a medal for Declamation, and in 1888 he won first prize for Debate. The picture below shows the medals.

S e r e n a wrote the following in her diary: "June 5, 1887: Monday 5th 'Commencement at Seminary' Evans 'Declaims' Got prize 'A Medal' (Stood good Examination also - Tuesday 7th End of Exams – Seminary closes"

In 1888, Evans was among the Gainesville Guard sent to Fernandina to quell a riot. The soldiers would bring the Yellow Fever back with them and set off the epidemic in Gainesville, but Evans did not get sick with the fever.

In September 1888, Serena wrote the following in her diary: "Thursday 6th 'Gainesville Guards ('sent to Fernandina to quell 'Riot' (Negroes) (Evans went)."

East Florida Seminary

In 1828, seven years after the United States bought the Territory of Florida from Spain, Governor William DuVal tried to have a college/seminary established, but it was not until 1851 that the General Assembly passed a bill to establish two seminaries in the state: one east of the Suwannee River (East Florida Seminary - EFS) and one west of the river (West Florida Seminary - WFS).

Two years later, Governor Thomas Brown signed a law that established Ocala as the site for EFS, Florida's first state-supported school of higher education.

The University of Florida traces its beginnings to that 1853 founding of EFS. In 1857, the Legislature established WFS in Tallahassee, and it would evolve into Florida State University.

The East Florida Seminary commencement in 1888

In the 1850s, 150 male residents of Alachua County petitioned the General Assembly to establish the East Florida Seminary at Newnansville, then the county seat.

However, when David Yulee's Florida Railroad, which was to link Fernandina and Cedar Key, bypassed Newnansville, county residents voted to create a new town along the railroad line and make it the county seat in 1853. They named it Gainesville in honor of Edmund P. Gaines, a general in the Seminole Indian War.

EFS moved to Gainesville in 1866, partly because of the presence of the railroad there, the fact that the town had the Gainesville Academy (a prospering secondary school), and because the seminary in Ocala closed during the War between the States because of a lack of funds. It is the school from which Evans Haile graduated (see previous pages).

EFS students in front of barracks in 1890s

EFS was to be a military school and an institution of secondary education, which many states in the South had before the war. The school emphasized military rules, not to prepare students for war, but to provide them with discipline. That is why Evans Haile is pictured in a military uniform.

*An engraving of the East
Florida Seminary
in Gainesville*

Another Haile died late that decade: Benjamin Haile, the fourth child of Thomas Evans and Serena Haile. He was born on March 13, 1852, in Camden, South Carolina (see the next page for the only picture available of Ben). In 1875 Rev. William J. McCormick married Ben and Rachel Denton.

Their first and only child, Elizabeth "Bessie" Serena Haile, was born to them in 1877 (see image to the right). According to Serena's diary, they had a farm to the east in Arredondo.

On October 3, 1889, Ben fell ill with nausea and fainting spells. As he grew worse, he was moved from his house to that of Mr. and Mrs. W.F. Rice. Mr. Rice was a prominent merchant in Arredondo. There he received an "Electropoise" treatment which appeared to relieve Ben's suffering. The Electropoise, however, was a piece of medical quackery, and, in fact, did absolutely nothing (see http://www.indiana.edu/~liblilly/blog/?p=1250).

Serena stayed at the Rices' house although Ben's brothers and sisters took turns sitting with him. Ben succumbed to his illness on October 10, 1889. The next day Serena wrote: "Friday 11th J(immie) & I went to A-(Arredondo) Ben looks natural – but oh that Cold 'Death' – J & I went to Church yard about the Grave Millie & children came – all followed him to his last resting place by John's side – Just at twilight."

Rev. A.B. Curry, pastor of Kanapaha Presbyterian Church, conducted the graveside service, where 'Christ the Rock of Ages' was sung.

Rachel Denton Haile (b. 1853) stayed close to the family and often served as the chaperone for many of the house parties which would be held at the Homestead. She died at 8 p.m. on February 23, 1912, at the home of her niece, Mrs. Norma B. Jordan, at Quincy, Florida. She had been visiting earlier with her sister-in-law (Mrs. Mary Budd) and her brother-in-law (William Edward Haile), both of Monticello, Florida. At the time of her death she resided on South Arredondo Street, Gainesville and was a member of the First Presbyterian Church.

This may be the only picture we have of Benjamin Haile. Ben was responsible for the oldest writing done on the interior walls of the house: 1859 - when he was just seven.

Bessie Haile (later Metz) with a friend, Guy Ulmer

74

Chapter Thirteen: 1890 to 1899

Esther Serena Chesnut Haile (pictured to the left) lived a long, productive 68 years, from May 31, 1827 until December 7, 1895.

Excerpts from Serena's diary, which ended in 1893, show us details from the early 1890s. What follows is a sample of some of those entries:

March 1890: [Serena Goes to the Dentist]:

"Monday 31st Clear & pleasant
J- came home in buggy about 10 A.M
(I went to Dentists – had
7 Teeth taken out – took
Chloroform – Evans went
with me – Dr Lancaster
there – Dr Cromwell pulled
them out – I went to Millie's
& had some quiet all day"

May 1890 [About the East Florida Seminary Graduation]
"Thursday 27th Clear A.M – I went to G'ville
in Train – commencing to rain just
after I got there – rained all day –
Stopped about dark – (I had to stay at
Millie's indoors) – I went at night to
'Seminary' Exercises – Amelia C &
Mea Dz & Enie all over there –"

75

"Prizes for 'Declamation' – Miss Phelps,
Mrs. Heyden & Dill<illegible> (Cadets) –
Chris. Matheson for 'Drill' (L<illegible> Boys'
Company) –
Wednesday 28th I went to 'Court House'
to 'Graduating Exercises' –
(A Crowd) – Amelia C, Mea & Chesnut all
dined at Millie's –
'Judge Raney' made address to Cadets & c-
Commenced to rain about 4 P.M
Rained on nearly all night – Sydney up
at G'ville, 'Ball' at Seminary"

The image to the left is of Serena in her middle age years, perhaps in her forties.

Feb. 22nd 1892: Serena sub-scribed to "LadiesWorld," "Womans Home Journal," "The House Circle" – all magazines

Feb 29th 1892: diary entry
"– I went P.O – Heard of death of "Columbus Haile Staunton, Va" - He was Thomas Haile's older brother.

Bennet Kelley and his wife, Mary Hodison Kelley, were living behind the Homestead in a cabin which had once been one of the 18 cabins where the enslaved people lived. In 1884 Serena had one of the cabins moved to a spot nearer the Homestead for Bennet and Mary to live in.

Serena recorded in her diary the death of Mary on February 20, 1892: "Saturday 20th ... Bennet's wife 'Mary' died about 4 P.M ('Grippe') ...   Sunday 21st Cloudy & Gloomy & Showery - got damp going to Church – ...(Bennet's wife buried in field in P.M)"

The "field" is a reference to the slave cemetery, the exact location of which cannot be determined. Based on oral tradition and research, a probable location, on private property, has been identified. However, nothing identifying it as a cemetery remains.

On June 4, 1892, Serena reported that Bennet had married Daphne S---. The name is illegible, but their marriage license reported her name as Daphne Summers. Daphne's death certificate in 1933 reported her father's name as Joe Debose.

The above picture of freedmen, Mr. and Mrs. Smith, includes Bennet, the younger man on the left.

A group photo from the 1890s that shows servants at a Haile House party - seated on the left is Bennet Kelley; seated on the right may be Bennet's father, Edmund. Daphne Kelley and Wm. Watts are standing on the right.

On October 9, 1892, Serena left for what would be her last trip to the city of her birth, Camden. Thomas did not go. She returned on Nov, 2, 1892, and made this summary entry in her diary: "I spent a pleasant time truly in Camden – saw many old friends – but not all I wanted to see ... went to Knights Hill Cemetery

"Oh how I was carried back to days of my childhood when my dear Father & Mother were living & to later years – after they were buried at that place!! – went 'Over the River' to Uncle Lawrence's old place to visit his remaining family – all so kind to me –"

Knights Hill Cemetery was the Chesnut family cemetery where her parents, grandparents, sister, brother, and famous aunt and uncle, diarist Mary Boykin Miller Chesnut and husband General James Chesnut Jr., among others, were laid to rest.

Other Hailes died that decade. James Chesnut Haile, called Jimmie by the family, was the sixth child of Thomas Evans and Serena Haile. Family records indicate Jimmie was born at Kanapaha on June 29, 1855, although the 1870 census states he was born in South Carolina. The 1880 census supports a Florida birth. He was never married and worked on the Haile farm all his life. He died of an unknown ailment in May 1891 and is buried in the family plot of the Kanapaha Church Cemetery. There are no known pictures of Jimmie at this time.

Another Haile who died in the 1890s was Thomas Evans Haile, who was born on May 31, 1824, in Camden, South Carolina. He married Esther Serena Chesnut (May 31, 1827 - Dec. 7, 1895), and they had fifteen children. Thomas Evans Haile died in December 1896 and is buried in the Kanapaha Church Cemetery.

Pictures of Thomas Evans Haile: as a young man
(on the left) and as an old man on the right

Another death that decade was Columbus Haile (pictured to the left), one of Thomas Haile's older brothers (they had the same mother). Columbus, who was called "Lum" by the family, lived from January 1820 to February 25, 1892. He married Ann "Louisa" McCaa (Aug 17, 1825 – May 6, 1905) on November 11, 1846; she was the sister of Charles E. Haile's wife, Elise McCaa Haile; and James Chesnut's wife, Amelia McCaa.

In 1876 he was accidentally shot by Eskine Miller and spent his remaining 16 years as an invalid. He died in 1892 and is buried in Staunton, VA. His obituary in the *Staunton Spectator* on March 2, 1892:

"HAILE- In this city at 3 o'clock, Thursday morning, Feb 25th, Mr. Columbus Haile, in his 73rd year of his age. He removed to this place about 20 years ago from Alabama. For sixteen years he had been an invalid – since he had been shot by mistake by M* Erskine Miller, He was a highly respected citizen. He left 4 daughters and 2 sons – Mrs. Donald Allen, of Texas, Mrs. Will N. Kinney, of West End, and Misses Katie and Lottie Haile, and two sons, Messrs. Columbus Haile of St. Louis, and Boykin Haile of Little Rock Arkansas. His funeral was from the Episcopal church Saturday afternoon Feb 27th. The pall bearers were: William A. Burnett, E.M. Cushing, J.M. Kinney, J.F. Tannehill, T.C. Elder, P.H. Trout and G.G. Child."

There were, then, three sisters who married into the Haile-Chesnut family: 1st, Ann Louisa McCaa married Columbus Haile, brother of Thomas Haile, and lived in Staunton, Virginia; 2nd, Elise McCaa married Charles Evans Haile, the brother of Thomas Haile, and moved to Florida; third, Amelia McCaa married James Chesnut, Serena's brother, and moved to Florida. Serena's own sister Mary was married to Thomas Haile's brother Edward until her death in Philadelphia in 1858. She was buried in the Old Quaker Cemetery in Camden.

Another Haile who died in the 1890s was John Haile, Thomas Haile's younger brother who moved to Alachua County. John was one four Haile brothers who moved to Alachua County: Thomas, John, Charles, and Edward - along with their mother Amelia.

John (pictured to the right) was the younger brother of Thomas Evans Haile and the son of Benjamin Haile Jr. and Benjamin's 2nd wife, Amelia Evans. John was the second youngest of Benjamin Haile's children. John, who was born November 11, 1833 (or 1832) in South Carolina, died October 21, 1897, in Richmond, Virginia. He is buried in Magnolia Cemetery, Charleston, SC, in the Gibbes' crypt. The cause of death: heart disease.

In 1857, he bought 960 acres from Mathew and Ann Hawkins and named the plantation San Felasco; it was located about seven miles southwest of Newnansville. In the War between the States he served with the 2nd Florida Cavalry CSA. John kept business ledgers for his San Felasco plantation which detailed how former slaves employed as workers were kept in debt.

This picture shows Bennet Kelley with his first wife, Mary Hodison Kelley. They married in 1876. According-
ing to Serena's diary, she died
of the grippe around 4 p.m. on Feb-
ruary 20, 1892. The diary says on
the next day, Feb 21, "Bennet's wife
buried in field in P.M." This mention
of a "field" is likely a reference to the
slave cemetery on the property.

To the right is an image of the
marriage license of Bennet Kelley
and Mary Hodison, who were
married on February 16, 1876,
by Rev. H. Haile.

82

Maud Graham (indicated with an arrow that someone put on the photo perhaps at the time) in 1897 in Daytona Beach

Maud Graham, pictured to the right in 1898, the daughter of James Madison Graham and Lydia Graham, was born in 1880 in Piedmont, West Virginia. Her father was a very prominent citizen in Gainesville having organized the First National Bank of Gainesville and served as its president for many years. Maud married Evans Haile, a prominent Gainesville defense attorney, on April 16, 1906. Maud preferred to live in the city so the Homestead was primarily used for house parties. She and Evans had two sons, Tommy and Graham. She was very active in social clubs; was a member of Holy Trinity Episcopal Church, the Order of the Eastern Star, Daughters of the American Revolution, and United Daughters of the Confederacy. She died in 1957 after an extended illness and was buried in Evergreen Cemetery in Gainesville. Her husband is buried in the Kanapaha Presbyterian Church Cemetery.

The Death of Serena Haile

Serena Haile died on Saturday, December 7, 1895, at the age of 68. "Her Last Repose" was a tribute in the *Gainesville Sun* on the next day. The funeral service took place at noon on December 8th at First Presbyterian Church. Her body was laid to rest near her sons in the Kanapaha Presbyterian Church Cemetery. (See the next page for a photo of her grave site.) Excerpts from "Her Last Repose" – Serena Haile's Obituary in the *Gainesville Sun*:

"Mrs. Thomas E. Haile, beloved wife of T.E. Haile, Sr. died last night at the residence of her son, Evans Haile, Esq. in the 70th year of her age. Deceased leaves a devoted husband, eight sons, two daughters and one brother, Capt. James Chesnut, to mourn her demise. Mrs. Haile was one of the oldest and most highly respected ladies of this section, and her death will be universally regretted. The funeral service will be held at the Presbyterian church to-day at 12 m., the remains being accompanied to Kanapaha cemetery by private conveyance. Rev. E.W. Way will conduct the services." – From *Gainesville Sun*, Dec. 8, 1895

From the *Gainesville Daily Sun*, December 10, 1895: "… The services were concluded by singing the beautiful hymn, 'Asleep in Jesus.' During the singing of this hymn there was hardly a dry eye in the congregation. All eyes seemed to be directed to the representatives of the large family grouped near the coffin and especially to the aged husband and father, whose head was bowed in grief. A silent tribute was paid to the deceased, whose earnest Christian work has characterized her entire life and who had assisted in rearing a large family, every living member of which stands high in the esteem of their associates… Probably no lady in Alachua county had a larger circle of acquaintances, and she was beloved by all who knew her for her many noble qualities of head and heart. She was a lady of whom it can truthfully be said that she enjoyed the respect, confidence and esteem of all who knew her. Her demise will be mourned not only by the surviving members of the family, but by hundreds of acquaintances in Florida and South Carolina whom during her long and useful life she had become endeared to. To the aged husband and the sons and daughters who are still living, the Sun would extend heartfelt condolences…"

Serena had died intestate and on October 12, 1896, son Walter K. Haile was appointed administrator of the estate by Judge H.G. Mason.

The grave stone of Serena Haile in the
Haile plot of the Kanapaha
Presbyterian Cemetery

The Death of Thomas Haile

Sometime after Serena's death, daughter Millie Taylor brought her father, Thomas Evans Haile Sr., to Tallahassee to live with them. He passed away there just before midnight on December 31, 1896. The following obituary appeared in the January 3, 1897 edition of the *Florida Times Union*:

"Thomas E. Haile.

A Refined and Intelligent Christian Gentleman Laid to Rest.

Arredondo, Fla., January 2. – The body of Mr. Thomas E. Haile was brought to Kanapaha yesterday on a special train from Tallahassee and laid away to rest in the Kanapaha cemetery by the side of his wife, who died a year ago. The body was accompanied by the family of the deceased: his sons, W. K. Haile, superintendent of the Southern Express company; C. M. Haile, trace clerk of the Southern Express company; Sydney Haile, F. C. & P., and L. W. and C. E. Haile of Kanapaha. Colonel Evans Haile, a prominent lawyer of Gainesville, and many friends from that place were also present. The body was taken from the train directly to the church, and the beautiful burial service of the Presbyterian church was there conducted by the Rev. Mr. Way, pastor of the Gainesville Presbyterian church. The pall-bearers were Mr. George E. Broome, Hon. J. A. Carlisle, member of the legislature; Col. H. G. Mason, County Judge; Col. Z. T. Taylor, ex-county judge; Messrs. R. Z. Tart and John Bartleson. Mr. Thomas Haile was a native of Kershaw county, South Carolina, and a typical representative of the old antebellum regime.

He was one of the largest and wealthiest planters of the old South, a large landholder, and the owner of many slaves. His home was all that cultivation, elegance and refinement combined with wealth could make it, and the princely hospitality which was so characteristic of the rich southern planter was lavishly dispensed to all. The results of the war left him poor, but, unbroken in spirit, and to the end of his long and useful life he was ever with the young a bright and pleasant companion.

He was a strikingly handsome man, of commanding figure and appearance, a great reader, and with a mind far above the average, he had stored it with much information. He was one of the pioneer settlers of this section of the country, having arrived here over forty years ago. Cultured, refined and intelligent, he was a Christian gentleman of the 'old school.' He had lived beyond his alloted three-score years and ten, and with the expiring old year, just twenty minutes to the beginning of the new, a long and useful life went out."

After Thomas Haile's move to Tallahassee, the Haile's son Lawrence and his wife lived at the Homestead for a short time. Thomas Haile also died intestate, and the Homestead and surrounding property eventually were acquired by Evans Haile.

The grave stone of Thomas Haile in the Haile plot of the Kanapaha Presbyterian Cemetery

Chapter Fourteen: 1900 to 1909

During this period Evans Haile, the fourteenth child and a defense attorney, acquired the house and property. He and his wife, Maud Graham (1880 – 1957), hosted parties at the vacant old plantation house. Some of Gainesville's most prominent citizens attended house parties, impromptu dances and picnics at the old Homestead. Many recorded their names on the walls of the Music Room and Parlor.

The local newspaper, *The Gainesville Star*, described one such party in 1905. Below is that excerpt for Friday, February 3, 1905:

"The Haile Homestead
A Spot of Natural Beauty and a Hospitable Retreat.

How would you like to visit one of the most hospitable homes in Florida? Would it not be a treat? Well, The Star will give its readers a pointer where one is located. If you go by rail it will be about fifteen minutes' ride; if by vehicle an hour and a half, depending largely on who is your traveling companion. About a mile and a half beyond Arredondo is situated one of the most beautiful homesteads of which the South can boast – the Haile homestead. The present owner, Mr. Evan[s] Haile, has improved and enlarged this delightful place of abode until its capacity has attained sufficient proportions to handsomely and easily accommodate a group of his friends to the number of fifty when the inclination possesses them to storm his premises.[continued on next page]

A copy of the newspaper article

87

[continuation of newspaper article]

At intervals of every thirty days and sometimes more frequently this true Southern gentlemen of the old school gives a house social party, which are the delight of many of his Gainesville friends as well as those from every section of the state. On these occasions there are generally about twenty-five ladies and gentlemen present. Dancing is the principal feature of pleasure indulged in. An unbleached orchestra, composed of four talented negroes, with rare ragtime skill on their instruments, is employed to furnish the music to enliven the occasions.

The piano is the instrument that furnishes the agency for many delightful and entertaining instrumental and vocal solos.

... seats are located all about the lawn, with hammock swings suspended from the majestic trees.

The appointments of this grand homestead are colonial, even to the servants, and rival those of old-time Southern days. The furniture is of beautiful antique pattern.

The homestead of Mr. Haile is ...." [The rest of the article is missing.]

The south wall of the Music Room has mention of an "Impromptu Dance" on May 18, 1904 - with mention of an Unbleached Orchestra.

Evans stocked the woods around the Homestead with quail and held weekend hunting parties for his friends. Quail, fox and turkey were among their favorite objectives.

As discussed in Chapter Eleven, Amelia E. "Millie" Haile, the Hailes' eldest daughter, married Robert Fenwick Taylor. She died on November 26, 1901, in Tallahassee, Florida and is buried in the family plot of Kanapaha Cemetery.

She married Judge Robert Fenwick Taylor on February 1, 1872, in a ceremony conducted by W.J. McCormick at Kanapaha Plantation.

On November 11, 1892, "Millie" Taylor moved with her husband and their children, Carl and Ena, to Tallahassee. Serena noted the sad leave-taking in her diary: "Friday 11th – ... Mr Taylor, Millie, Ena & Carl left on 'F.C. & P' R.R- at '11.16' for Jax – to spend night & then for Tallahassee on Saturday. Even Horse & Buggy [were] put in 'Baggage & Freight Car' – It was a sad 'Leave taking' – we are 'broken up.'"

Their unnamed infant daughter died right after birth on August 9, 1876, and is buried in the family plot of the Kanapaha Cemetery. (See photo to the right of the baby's grave site.)

Serena "Ena" Haile Taylor, the daughter of Millie and Judge Taylor, was born August 21, 1878, married Judge William Hull Ellis on April 17, 1906, in Tallahassee, and died November 28, 1956 at the home of her daughter Amelia (Mrs. James Whitehurst) in Brooksville, Florida. She is also buried in the family plot at the Kanapaha Cemetery. (About the name of Serena: Her grave marker says Serena Taylor Ellis, but in the Family Bible it says Serena Haile Taylor.)

A newspaper article dated December 29, 1905, described Judge Taylor's announcement of the betrothal: "In conservance with this time honored custom I now, here in this dear old home of her mother, around which cluster so many sacredly tender memories, proclaim and announce the marriage engagement of my daughter, Ena, to Hon. William H. Ellis, Florida's distinguished Attorney General, the marriage to take place in April next, 'when the roses come again.'"

The wedding was attended by Gov. and Mrs. Broward, as well as former governors William Bloxham and William Jennings.

Governors Broward   *and Bloxham*   *and Jennings*

The photo above is of a party held on March 1, 1903. The people on the left are left to right: Lois Hale (NOT Haile - not related), Eva Haile (later married J.B. Dell Jr.) - she was the daughter of Charles Evans Haile and Elise McCaa Haile; Joe E. Hall, Eula Denton, and Lee Graham.

The group on the right are left to right: Ben Thrower, May Zell, Henry Davis, Evans Haile, Maud Graham (who would marry Evans in 1906), Louise Zell, and J.B. Dell (who would marry Eva Haile in 1906).

In this photo one can see the kitchen on the right/east side and the cistern on the left/west side of the house.

The University of Florida

The first decade of the 20th century was very important in the history of the
University of Florida, a school that would
see many Hailes and their descendants
enroll over the years. Gainesville already
had the East Florida Seminary (see Chap-

ter Twelve). In 1884, education officials established in Lake City
north of Gainesville the Florida Agricultural College (FAC), the
state's first land-grant college. Above is a picture of a building at
FAC.

In 1905, the Legislature passed the Buckman Act, which
merged Gainesville's East Florida Seminary, Lake City's FAC, St.
Petersburg's Normal and Industrial School, and Bartow's South
Florida Military College into the new University of the State of
Florida, a name later shortened to the University of Florida.

That same year, the Board of Control chose to move the
school to Gainesville. In September 1906, the school began hold-
ing its first classes on the Gainesville campus.

A very early picture of UF when it first moved to Gainesville

Examples of writing on the walls of the Haile Homestead
by students/cadets from the East Florida Seminary

Students/cadets from the East Florida Seminary (EFS) may have been visiting the Haile Homestead, perhaps to visit their former classmate, Evans Haile, or his older brother Sydney Haile, who also attended EFS, when they wrote on the walls of the house, as was the custom at that time at the Haile Homestead.

They may have been with their parents or older siblings who were part of the party crowd with whom Evans ran.

From the sample of a segment of the "Talking Walls" pictured on the upper left of this page, the date seems to have been (19)03.

Evans Haile would have dressed like these cadets
at the Florida Agricultural College in Lake City.

Of the three couples pictured here in the 1900s,
Maud and Evans are on the far right,
and Lee Graham is in the center, first row.

94

Chapter Fifteen: 1910 to 1919

Pictured to the left is an image of Serena's brother James Chesnut (1835 - 1916), who moved to Alachua County in 1861. His plantation was on County Road 241 north of Jonesville. Pictured with him is his wife, Amelia Boykin McCaa Chesnut. She was the sister of Charles Evans Haile's wife, Elise McCaa Haile, and Columbus Haile's wife, Ann "Louisa" McCaa Haile.

After fighting in the War between the States, James was mustered out in 1863. He continued with farming and cotton until 1912. He and Amelia moved to Gainesville to live with their daughter, Mrs. Jordan. He is buried in Evergreen Cemetery, Gainesville.

His obituary in *The Gainesville Sun* had this: "Capt. James Chesnut, Sr., one of the first settlers of Alachua county and one of the most esteemed citizens of the State, passed away Tuesday at 10 o'clock a.m. at the home of his daughter, Mrs. B. F. Jordan, 401 Oak avenue, north. Until a few weeks ago Capt. Chesnut was in his usual good health but he contracted lagrippe which, owing to his advanced age, brought about complications which the best medical skill and the most loving and careful attention could not withstand. Capt. Chesnut would have reached his eighty-first birthday had he lived until Friday of the present week."

This 1916 photo, which is owned by Evans Haile, shows Thomas Evans Haile and James Graham Haile Sr., the sons of Evans and Maud Haile.

This photo from around 1917 shows Tommy and Graham (l,r) on the horse, along with Maud Haile and Bennet Kelley.

96

Chapter Sixteen: 1920 to 1929

One of the Hailes who died in the 1920s was Walter Kennedy Haile (1862 – 1920 - seen here to the right).

Born on June 30, 1862, in Kanapaha, he was the eleventh child of Thomas Evans and Serena Haile.

He attended East Florida Seminary, then the Virginia Military Institute, where he graduated in 1883.

In 1884, he worked as a clerk with the Southern Express Company at Cedar Key(s), Florida, and in the same year was made "express messenger" on the Florida Railway and Navigation Company.

In 1886, he was promoted to an "important office Clerkship" and in 1887 was appointed agent at Cedar Key(s); the next year he was promoted to Route Agent.

In 1887, he married Leontine Lockett of Cedar Key(s) in that town (see next page for a possible photo of her). In 1896, the same year that his father died, Walter was appointed superintendent of the Southern Express Company at Jacksonville.

Young Walter was a Democrat, a member of the Episcopal Church, the Seminole Club, and "the Country Club." He was also a member of the Jacksonville Board of Trade, serving on the Board of Governors and also vice-president of the Board of Trade beginning in 1902.

Pictured to the right may be Leontine, Walter's wife.

He also served as Director in the People's Bank and Trust Company for three years; director in the Florida Life Insurance Company for two years; vice-president of the Metropolitan Investment Company; and president of the Metropolitan Improvement Company.

On March 22, 1920, while living at 1540 Post Street in Jacksonville, he died of pneumonia. He is buried in Evergreen Cemetery, Lot 148, Section H.

One of his obituaries noted that he was "broad-minded, liberal and progressive, and believes in encouraging enterprise and attracting investment." He believes this can best be done by means of "liberal laws in all states for large corporations, inducing investments of capitalists in the States needing development, with national government supervision to a reasonable extent. He believes that it will be helpful in every one's life to 'be just and fair to all. Learn, first, to control yourself before attempting to control others. Always hear both sides of the question.' Mr. Haile does not believe in sumptuary legislation, and considers it useless to attempt to legislate temperance or morality into people."

*This photo of two girls on horseback and a man standing
was also taken in 1926 in front of a barn and stable.*

This photo, also from 1926, shows the kitchen in the yard.

99

*This photo of the Homestead in 1926 shows three people
on the south side of the northeast corner of the house.
One can see the kitchen on the far right,
then a very small building, and then the larger smoke house.*

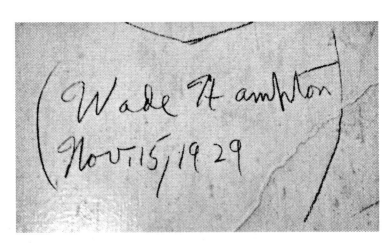

*W. Wade Hampton III, the son of Wade Hampton Jr. and a local attor-
ney in Gainesville, wrote on the walls of the Homestead as a 14-year-
old in 1929. He also indicated that the Hailes hid blackberry wine at
the Homestead during Prohibition. When his granddaughter brought
him to see the Homestead shortly before he died, he showed where he
had written on the south wall of the Music Room.*

*This picture taken in 1926 shows Charles's wife (Annie Morgan Haile)
the second from left. Others in the picture are, left to right,
Lee Graham Jr. to her right and Maud Graham Haile,
and Mrs. Lee Graham Sr. to her left.*

*Another photo showing unidentified people at a party
in the early 1900s at the Haile Homestead*

The Patterson Community Cemetery

Karen Kirkman, co-author of this book, wrote the following for the Alachua County Commission in 2006:

"The land to the south of Arredondo station was once part of a large plantation owned by Lewis J. Patterson of South Carolina. While he and his wife, Hannah Margaret, are not listed on the 1860 Alachua County census (they are found on the Kershaw County, South Carolina census), his name does appear on the 1860 Schedule 2 of Slave Inhabitants for Alachua County as the owner of 28 enslaved persons. His property was sold by the sheriff at a bankruptcy sale in 1869.

The large tract of land included 539 acres of Section 22, Township 10, Range 19. This area is noted on an 1877 plat map as 'Patterson Land.' It is in this area where the Patterson Community Cemetery lies.

The Patterson Community Cemetery

The cemetery is found at the end of SW 49th Street, an unpaved road scarred by deep ruts that runs past at least three old cottages. The cemetery has several unusual markers, one of which is shaped like a duck's head (see photo below).

While the lives and relationships of the people buried there deserve more research, we discovered the grave of one Edmund Kelley Jr., his wife Lizzie and their daughter Mathilda (see photo of the grave site on the next page).

Census data show that Edmund Kelley Jr. was the son of Edmund and Charity Kelley, who were enslaved at the Kanapaha plantation of Thomas and Serena Haile.

Edmund Jr. was born a free man in 1869. There is a five-acre piece of land immediately to the east of the present day Kanapaha Presbyterian Church property and fronting Archer Road that remains in the Kelley family.

103

Depressions/indentations in the ground throughout the cemetery indicate that further research will probably find unmarked graves there.

In 2014 the property was still owned by Edmund Kelley Jr.'s grandchildren, the family having refused to sell when approached by developers. The Kelleys' father, also named Edmund, is buried with their mother in the Patterson Cemetery.

The property came into the possession of the family through Oliver Stinson in 1907. Mr. Stinson, who purchased the land for $150 from T.J. Swearingen in 1907, was married to Mathilda Kelley, a daughter of Edmund Kelley Jr.

By the 1910 census, Mathilda was listed as a widow, living with her parents and employed by a local family as a cook. In September of 1910 Mathilda sold the five-acre piece to her father for $20.

The Patterson Community Cemetery is deserving of more research. Many graves, obvious from depressions in the ground, are either unmarked or marked by now-illegible stones or funeral home markers."

The grave site of Edmund Kelley, Jr., Bennet's brother -
this grave site is at the cemetery.

105

Another Haile who died in this decade was Thomas Haile's brother, Charles Evans Haile (pictured to the right from his 1856 Princeton University yearbook). Born in Camden, South Carolina, on December 11, 1835, he was the youngest of the Haile brothers who moved to Florida.

Sometime in the late 1850s he moved to Alachua County and in 1859 purchased 800 acres of land. The 1860 census indicates he initially lived with his mother, Amelia, on her plantation, west of Gainesville. Roderick Cameron, a Scot, is shown as their overseer. When war broke out, Charles returned to South Carolina and initially served the Confederacy, first as a private with the Kirkwood Rangers, Company H, 7th South Carolina Cavalry Regiment, and then as a courier for Brigadier General Finnegan in Florida.

In 1866 after he and Elise McCaa were married in South Carolina, they returned to Florida to farm and raise a family. In 1867 their first child, Charles Evans Haile Jr. was born on their plantation. Other children would soon follow: Elise McCaa Haile (1868), John "Jack" McCaa Haile (1870), Amelia Boykin Haile (1871), James "Cullie" Chesnut Haile (1873), Louisa McCaa Haile (1876) who would marry John Chesnut, the son of Thomas and Helen Chesnut, Eva Haile (1879), who would marry James Blaxton Dell, and Withers "Allen" Haile (1882). Eva Haile Dell and two of her sisters-in-law would be among the founding members of the Gainesville Chapter, Daughters of the American Revolution in 1922 (see page 162). Elise Haile died at home in January 1887. Charles, who remained a farmer the rest of his life, died at the home of his son, C.E. Haile Jr. in Live Oak, Florida, on August 14, 1924.

Chapter Seventeen: 1930 to 1939

The decade of the 1930s saw the death of several Hailes, for example, Mary Chesnut Haile (1859 - 1938), the 9th child of Thomas and Serena Haile. She married Josiah T. Budd II on March 24, 1881. To the right is a picture of Mary Budd on her honeymoon in 1881.

The thirteenth child of Thomas and Serena Haile, George Reynolds Haile, also died that decade. George (pic-

tured to the left) was born on December 20, 1865 at Kanapaha. The 1880 census takers found him living at home.

On December 27, 1887, he married Margaret "Maggie" Ulmer Alston (1870 – 1939) in a double ring ceremony officiated by Rev. A.B. Curry at Kanapaha Presbyterian Church (brother Lawrence Whitaker and Olivia Sutherland Dawson were married at the same time).

During the Yellow Fever Epidemic of 1888, when Gainesville was quarantined, George became sick with an unidentified fever.

George and Maggie (pictured to the left) were living in Belleview, Florida at the time. Maggie's father, a doctor, was tending to George.

Serena's diary entry from December 15, 1888, says: "Sat 15th I left home Friday night 14th 10 P.M from Arredondo, for 'Belleview' – A very cold, clear night – got to Waldo at '1 A.M. – staid there until '8' P.M, 19 hours!! got to 'Belleview' 12 M - found George very ill –Dr. Alston there–"

George bounced back almost as soon as his mother came, and Serena felt comfortable enough with George's recovery to return home for Christmas on December 23rd.

In the following years George and Maggie started their family: Alston Reynolds Haile (b. 1889), Esther Fenwick Haile (b. 1890), Miriam Penfield Haile (b. 1892), Marguerite Ulmer Haile (b. 1895), and George Evans Haile (born September 14, 1901 and died October 3, 1901, at Tallulah Lodge, GA).

The elder three children were christened at Kanapaha Presbyterian Church in April 1893, as Serena's diary relates: "Sunday 2nd a beautiful day - 'Mr Curry' came P.M 'Cristenal' at Church – 'Alston Reynolds' 'Esther Fenwick' – 'Miriam Penfield' (George & Maggie's children) 'James Gibbes' (W. & Edna C's Baby) – all behaved nicely –"

In 1900 George was a railroad agent, living in Leesburg, Florida. By 1910 the family was in Lake City, Florida, where George worked as a traveling salesman. In 1913 they made their final move to Jacksonville.

In 1920 George was selling soap for a living. The 1930 census for Jacksonville lists both George and Maggie as retired. George died on March 28, 1934, and was buried in Oaklawn Cemetery, Jacksonville. His obituary said he was a member of Riverside Presbyterian Church, a Mason, and a member of the Knights of Pythias.

Another death that decade was that of Evans Haile (1869 - 1934), the fourteenth child of Thomas and Serena Haile and a popular defense attorney in Gainesville who had acquired the Homestead and surrounding land.

This photo shows Evans Haile as the third person from the left; the men are in front of the Haile law firm in Gainesville.

Evans Haile (pictured to the right) died on December 3, 1934. His obituary in the Gainesville newspaper had these details:

"Evans Haile, widely known criminal lawyer of this section died at his home about 10:20 a.m. yesterday from an acute heart attack following an illness which had lasted for more than a year.

His health had apparently improved during the last few months, and he was able to return to his practice in a limited way. He represented several clients at the term of the circuit court which closed here last Friday.

Born and reared at the plantation of his parents, the late Thomas Evans Haile and Esther Serena Chesnut Haile, at Kanapaha, Mr. Haile built a career on friendships.

He was perhaps as widely known as any man in the county, and was surpassed by none in his knowledge of the intimate history of the people of the county in every generation since the days of the Reconstruction."

His obituary also had these details: "[Mr. Evans Haile was a] "lifelong worker in the Democratic party, ... was chairman of the county committee and a member of the state committee at the time of his death ... witnessed and took an active role in the battle to free Florida from the yoke of Reconstruction.

"One of his last acts was to collect the photographs of the negro and carpet bagger officials who held sway before the return of the Democrats to power;" "he rarely questioned a witness and almost never made a speech to a jury. His task was generally to advise with the lawyers handling the trial of the cases and to pick juries. Mr. Haile had not complained yesterday morning, but had eaten breakfast as usual and was at his home when death claimed him. He had been to the old Haile Plantation at Kanapaha Sunday as was his custom, and has been down town as usual on Saturday.

He was 65 years old, having been born June 11, 1869. His parents moved here from Camden, S.C., and were among the pioneer settlers of this section of Florida.

The couch in the downstairs parlor is a Duncan Phyfe sofa that belonged to Thomas Evans Haile's mother, Amelia Haile (who also moved to Alachua County). This sofa was donated to the HHH by Mary Budd Holmes, a granddaughter of Mary Chesnut Haile Budd, who was a daughter of Thomas and Serena Haile. Her cousin, Chesnut Budd Gearing (also a granddaughter of Mary Chesnut Haile Budd), paid to have the sofa recovered.

Continuation of the obituary for Evans Haile: "Still rejoicing in the glories of the old South, Mr. Haile clung to them at frist (sp) hand by his regular visits to the old Haile plantation at Kanapaha which his father and mother founded after they moved here as pioneers from Camden, S.C. It was there that he was born and reared, and it is near there, in the old Kanapaha Cemetery, that he will be buried today. His last visit was made on the day before he died."

"He married Miss Maud Graham in Gainesville April 18, 1906. She survives him as do their two sons, James Graham Haile and Thomas Evan[s] Haile, both students at the University of Florida."

Also surviving Mr. Haile are four brothers, W.E. Haile, Winter Garden; L.W. Haile, Miami; Sydney Haile, Ocala and C.M. Haile, Jacksonville; and one sister, Mrs. J.T. Budd of Quincy.

Funeral services for Mr. Haile will be held this afternoon at

2 o'clock at the First Presbyterian Church with Dr. U.S. Gordon, the pastor, officiating. Interment will follow in the Kanapaha Cemetery.

Another Haile who died that decade was Charles Evans Haile (pictured to the left) (1861 - 1934), Thomas and Serena's son (not Thomas's brother)."

Charles was the tenth child of Thomas Evans and Serena Haile. He married Annie Morgan Hayes, daughter of Judge Hayes of Alabama, on January 11, 1893.

They had no children. Charles is buried in the family plot in the Kanapaha Cemetery.

Another Haile, Sydney, died in 1938. Sydney (1864 - 1938) was the twelfth child of Thomas and Serena Haile. The image below is of Sydney as a relatively young man.

J. C. Littler, - Gainesville, Fla.

Sydney lived in town with his Aunt Millie and Uncle Fen Taylor while attending East Florida Seminary. During his last semester at school, he became seriously ill and returned to Kanapaha, where his parents nursed him back to health.

Still too ill to attend commencement exercises, he received his EFS diploma at home three days later on June 8, 1887.

On May 22, 1894, he married Natalie Venable (pictured to the left) of Farmville, Virginia, in Leesburg, Florida. The following March of 1895 they welcomed their first child: Marie Chesnut Haile.

At the time of his father's death in 1896, Sydney was working for the F.C. & P. Railroad.

The family moved to Lake City. Four children would follow, all born in Lake City, Florida: Vernon Venable Haile (b. Dec 6, 1902; d. May 2, 1904); twins: Mea (Amelia) Dozier Haile and Emilie Miller Haile, born Dec. 21, 1903; and Genevieve Venable Haile, born January 28, 1905.

Sometime in the 1900s the family moved to Ocala, Florida, where Sydney was employed as a railroad agent. According to writing done by Natalie on the back of a picture of the Homestead, Sydney lived at the Homestead from 1915-1918.

According to descendants Ann and Hunter Davis, he lived there to recuperate from an unknown condition. At the Haile family reunion on May 7, 2011, Ann Davis of Texas said that Sydney tried to convince Bennet and Daphne Kelley to move to Ocala with him in 1918.

Perhaps Bennet was exhibiting signs of dementia because Sydney thought Bennet would end up in Chattahoochee Mental Hospital, but the Kelleys would not go. Bennet did end up in Chattahoochee Mental Hospital, but not until 1933.

By 1920 Sydney was manager of a crate or box mill. A census done in 1935 showed Sydney (age 70), Natalie (63) and daughter Emilie (25) living at 403 E. Oklawaha Avenue in Ocala.

The census showed all three of them as having had four years of college; and Sydney as a retired accountant. Emilie was a stenographer.

Sydney as an older man lived in Ocala, Florida.

Sydney died on December 12, 1938. Natalie died on September 17, 1954. Both are buried together in Highland Memorial Park, Ocala, Florida.

The twin daughters of Sydney and his wife, Natalie Venable, were born in 1903: Mea (Amelia) Dozier Haile and Emilie (Emmie) Miller Haile.

The Haile family about 1938 in Ocala FL
Sitting (left to right) Genevieve Haile Kenny (daughter of Sydney and
Natalie Haile) with Natalie on her lap; Emilie Haile (who later mar-
ried Glenn Caldwell) (daughter of Sydney and Natalie Haile); Syd-
ney Haile; Natalie Venable Haile; Amelia Dozier Haile Lingenfelter
(daughter of Sydney and Natalie Haile) – with Mea (Mimi) on her lap.
Standing (left to right): Gregory Little Kenny; Ann Lingenfalter;
Harry Gelespie Kinnard (Sonny); Marie Haile Kinnard (daughter of
Sydney and Natalie Haile) ; Crenshaw Kinnard (Sonny – Boy), Paul
Nevin Lingenfelter, Jr.; Paul Nevin Lingenfelter, Sr.

The decade of the 1930s also saw the boarding up and closing of the Haile Homestead. It would remain "shuttered" until the 1970s, when it became the setting for the filming of the Marjorie Kinnan Rawlings short story entitled "Gal Young'un" (see Chapter 21). Fortunately, because the original Hailes had built the house so well, using cypress and heart of pine, it weathered through the decades well.

The brace-frame construction along with its mortise and tenon joinery, which was an antiquated method of joining pieces of wood, allowed the house to age well in the harsh conditions of north-central Florida.

The picture above shows the mortise and tenon joinery.
One can also see the axe (or adze) marks
from where the enslaved laborers trimmed the beams.

Another death of a Haile that decade greatly affected Serena. William "Willie" Edward Haile, the seventh child of Thomas Evans and Serena Haile, was born at Kanapaha on February 10, 1857. He died in 1935. Both the 1870 and 1880 census show him living at home, where he first worked for his father, and then in 1878 went to work for his uncle, Charles Evans Haile. After four years of managing his uncle's plantation, he moved to Ellenton, Florida, where he became a grower and shipper of vegetables. Two years later he drove a mail route between Tampa and Palmetto, traveling 50 miles per day, six days a week.

After one year he returned to Gainesville, where he worked as a merchant. In late 1885 he moved to Monticello, Florida, where his sister, Mary Haile Budd, lived. His brother-in-law, Josiah Budd II, hired him at his store, J.T. Budd & Son. On June 26, 1889, he married Margaret "Maggie" B. Turnbull (1866-1893) at Monticello, Florida. They had one child, Junius Turnbull Haile, born June 13, 1890.

This could be a photo of Maggie Turnbull Haile since it is dated in the 1880s.

On April 10, 1893, Serena received terrible news: "Monday 10th – ... At 12 M – Such a Shock !!! Evans sent Telegram Willie's wife Maggie died this A.M 4 O'clock, Monticello Oh I feel for my dear child! Monday 10th ... Oh the trouble at Monticello My dear Willie's sorrow!!!"

Maggie was buried in Roseland Cemetery, Monticello, in a plot owned by her father. On October 28, 1896, Willie married Adele "Nonnie" Lawrence Tatum (1875-1958).

They had two children: Esther Serena Haile Connolly (b. 1897) and Adaline Denham Haile (b. 1899).

The 1900 census shows Willie as a salesman in a general store. He opened his own grocery and seed store in Monticello. Their home in Monticello was on 325 E. Jefferson Street.

Two interior views of the Haile and West store in Monticello

In the 1920s they moved to Leesburg and opened the Leesburg Seed and Feed Company. The name was later changed to the Haile Seed and Feed Company.

Willie died on February 11, 1935, in Winter Garden, Florida. He was buried in Roseland Cemetery, Monticello. When his second wife, Nonnie, died in 1958, she was buried alongside him.

Chapter Eighteen: 1940 to 1969

We're going to combine the decades of the 1940s, 1950s, and 1960s because the house was shuttered and mostly unused during that time. Most of this information comes from the recollections of James "Graham" Haile Jr., the grandson of Evans and Maud Haile.

The picture here shows Evans and Maud's sons in the U.S. Army in Europe during World War II: James Graham Haile Sr. (Graham) on the right and Thomas Evans Haile (Tom) on the left.

121

One of the Hailes who died in the 1940s was Lawrence Whitaker Haile (1858 – 1945), the eighth child of Thomas Evans and Serena Haile. Lawrence, pictured below in 1894, spent his adult life as a clerk for various businesses on the east coast of Florida.

He finally settled in the Miami area, where he was a clerk at Baker & Holmes Co., FEC Railway, and Robert L. Edens Seed Company. The 1940 census shows him as a retired clerk.

He had married Olivia Sutherland Dawson in 1887 in a double ceremony with his brother (George Reynolds Haile) and Maggie Alston. Rev. A.B. Curry performed the wedding at Kanapaha Presbyterian Church. Olivia, whom Serena called "Olive" in her diary, died in Ocala, Florida, in 1893.

Their children were, first, Ralph Whitaker Haile (1888 – 1936), who worked as a bookkeeper in a saw mill in Dade County and who also served in the military during World War I, serving overseas from July 31, 1918 until April 29, 1919, before being discharged on May 20, 1919 as a private 1st class and as 10% disabled.

The second child of Olivia and Lawrence Whitaker Haile was Lawrence "Laurie" Dawson Haile (1891 – 1956), who served in World War I and later worked as a bank clerk in Titusville, Florida.

He is buried in Eau Gallie Cemetery, Eau Gallie, Florida.

After Olivia died in December 1893, Lawrence Haile married Mary Louise Bauskett of Miami, Florida, on June 17, 1896, at the residence of Captain J.A. Carlisle, Reverend W.W. Way officiating. (Pictured above is Mary L. Bauskett Haile, Lawence's second wife.)

They resided at Kanapaha right after the wedding, and he served as a postmaster at Kanapaha from February 18, 1896 until March 4, 1898.

The 1900 census listed him as a clerk in the FEC Hotel Office in St. Augustine, Florida. Their children were Mary Louise Taylor Haile (b. 1897) and Dorethea (Dorothy) Chesnut Haile (b. 1899).

Recollections of Graham Haile

In the late 1930s, Graham Haile's father, James Graham Haile Sr. (the son of Evans and Maud Haile) and his uncle, Tom (Thomas Evans Haile, the son of Evans and Maud Haile) put a tin roof on the Homestead.

A picture of the house with its tin roof

In that decade, Graham, who was born in 1943, started hunting on the Haile Homestead property with his dad at the age of 7 with a BB gun. They mostly hunted for quail and squirrel.

The woods were not terribly thick around the Homestead then, consisting mostly of blackjack oak and pine, and therefore were clear enough to spot animals. Graham still remembers a pecan tree and a sour orange tree there.

Mr. Deas lived catty corner across Archer Road from the front gate of the Haile Homestead. He had a two-story farm house there. He leased the Haile land and ran cattle on the property from the 1940s through the 1960s. Every year Mr. Deas would burn part of the property to keep the scrub down. There was a cattle dipping vat on the property.

Graham, who received his first 20-gauge shotgun in 1952, used it for quail hunting. He lived on 8th Avenue in Gainesville and remembers riding his bike, with the shotgun lying on the handlebars, all the way to the Homestead. During those decades his dad had wood cut down and sold for making light poles.

Maud Graham, the wife of Evans Haile, lived from 1880 to 1957. Pictured here as a little girl, she married Evans Haile on April 18, 1906.

An old black man, Dewey Strong, was living in a cabin behind the Homestead in what used to be Bennet Kelley's house. Dewey, who was born in 1899, walked all bent over, a posture that scared some people, according to Graham.

The property had lots of rattlesnakes. One person told Graham about finding one that was two feet high when all coiled up.

Graham also saw a picture of one killed on the property that was 8-9 feet long. Dewey said that the rattling of the rattlesnakes under his house sometimes kept him up all night.

The Homestead needed a caretaker because college students were always coming out to the house to create mischief and because some thought that the place was haunted. Dewey would go out and chase them off with a shotgun, but once the trespassers actually assaulted Dewey. Graham remembered seeing Dewey's injured eye.

Trespassers sometimes stole the Homestead's original furniture. Graham remembered going into a local antique store and seeing some of the furniture for sale, but he could never prove that it had come out of the Homestead. Some people cut a hole in the floor and got into the Homestead through the hole. Graham remembers some steel beds that his dad gave to Mr. Deas, along with some other furniture. Unfortunately, Mr. Deas's house burned down.

Graham remembered an old crank telephone in the house, but it too was stolen. Some of the furniture was given to family members over time, and other pieces were in good enough condition to be used in the Homestead when it opened in 2001. The Historic Haile Homestead (HHH), Inc. still has some pieces in storage awaiting funds to restore them.

The piano that is covered with a cloth and used as a table in the front passage - see next page for more about this piano.

At one time there were four square grand pianos in the Homestead. Two are there now. One is being used as a table.

An original Bacon and Raven piano (built between 1841 and 1855) was restored as a display piece and in 2012 was donated to the Homestead by children of Eloise and Graham Haile Sr.: Graham Haile Jr., Evans Haile, and Beverly Haile Parrish.

The original Bacon and Raven piano in the house today

In the early 1950s (1950 – 1953) Graham remembers that his daddy hired three African-American men that he understood to be descendants of enslaved people at the Homestead. They planted 50,000 little pine trees on the property.

During his hunting expeditions, Graham remembers following an old road to the north and coming across a huge sawdust pile, where there had been a saw mill. He also remembers an old shack whose interior walls were lined with pages of Sears Roebuck catalogues from the early 1900s. Mr. Lamar Taylor, son of M.A. Taylor (or Toby Taylor), the caretaker hired in the 1970s, recalls that house as belonging to a Mrs. Nash.

Notes about the caretaker Dewey Strong by Karen Kirkman: Dewey appears on the 1930 census, age 31 (b. in 1899 in South Carolina). He is recorded as "Caretaker of Plantation." He is living next to the Taylors (M.A. Taylor's parents). Based on census research Dewey's real name may have been Melvin Dewey Strong. In the 1920 census he is shown living in Fairbanks, Florida, as a farm laborer. This means that he was hired as caretaker in the 1920s. By that time Bennet Kelley, who was born in 1844 and died in 1933, was a very old man so the Hailes needed a new caretaker. Melvin Dewey Strong (July 7, 1899 – June 6, 1956) is buried in the Odd Fellows Cemetery, Starke, Florida.

This dilapidated shack may have been the caretaker's house.

Chapter Nineteen: 1970 to 1979

The decade of the 1970s saw the Historic American Building Survey done; also the filming and release of "Gal Young Un."

The movie poster for "Gal Young Un" that showed Mattie and Trax

In 1976, Victor Nunez of Tallahassee filmed a Marjorie Kinnan Rawlings' 1932 short story entitled "Gal Young Un" in Alachua County and partly at the Haile Homestead.

It is the story of how a young moonshiner, Trax Colton, won the heart of a country woman, Mattie Syles, during Prohibition, but then brought to Mattie's house his paramour, Elly. The subsequent film of the same name as the story was well received, for example, at the 1980 Cannes Film Festival in France. The film had several showings in Gainesville, where many local actors in the film resided, for example as a fundraiser for the old post office, which became the Hippodrome Theater.

The cast for the "Gal Young Un" movie was as follows:

Mattie – Dana Preu
Trax – David Peck
Elly – J. Smith
Storekeeper - Gene Densmore
Edna –Jennie Stringfellow
Blaine – Tim McCormack
Jeb Lantry – Casey Donovan
Eddy Lantry – Mike Garlington
Edgar – Marshal New
Phil – Bruce Cornwell
Winner at cards – John Pieters
Other bootlegger – Gil Lazier
Other bootlegger's girl – Tina Moore
Hotel manager – Marc Glick
Girl in orange – Kerry McKenney

Mary at store – Sarah Drylie Turpentine heckler – Randy Ser People at store – Bernie Cook, Mr. Lewis Ivey, Mrs. Lewis Ivey, Fred Wood, Sissy Wood People at party – Billie Henry, J.D. Henry (JD is on the HHH Inc., Board of Directors and is the great grandson of Charles Evans Haile), Susan Holzer, Brian Lietz Still builders – Pat Garner, Gus Holzer, Ross Sturlin

This outhouse on the property was built for the movie.

130

Chapter Twenty: 1980 to 1989

The decade of the 1980s saw the Haile family reunion, as well as the placing of the House on the National Register of Historic Places (1986).

In communications with co-author Karen Kirkman in June, 2014, James "Graham" Haile Jr. wrote the following regarding the 1982 Haile family reunion: "Mom did the majority of the work. Folks were aging and she wanted to get the whole family involved with the restoration if possible." Plus it was the 40th wedding anniversary of Graham Sr. and his wife, Eloise. "Mom, Tom, and the Alachua Conservation Trust (ACT) were involved in getting it on the historic place records and in raising funds for restoration. They found out politics played a big role and even tried to get the state to take it over and do the restoration at one point."

This photo shows James Graham Haile Sr. (1912 - 1984), son of Evans and Maud Haile, on the steps of the Homestead in the 1970s or 1980s.

131

At the first Haile family reunion in 1982, Dana Preu, who played Mattie in the "Gal Young Un" movie that was filmed at the Haile Homestead in the 1970s, signed posters of the movie.

The family put up this sign on Archer Road during the reunion.

Those who attended the first family reunion, May 15, 1982, posed for a group photo on the steps of the house.

According to Graham Haile Jr., Tom donated his half interest in the Homestead to the Alachua Conservation Trust (ACT), perhaps for tax reasons, and was not interested in staying involved since he was living in North Carolina with his new wife. As trustee of his parents' estates, Graham wanted to keep involved, as did his brother Evans and sister Beverly. The family reunion was held on May 15, 1982 at the Historic Haile Homestead.

Eloise Smith Haile (1920 - 1996) with the help of her husband, James Graham Haile Sr., organized the event. Eloise was the mother of James Graham Haile Jr., Beverly Haile Parrish (currently on the HHH Board of Directors), and (Samuel) Evans Haile. Dana Preu, star of the movie "Gal Young Un," and the Gus Holzer family (who was part of the filming crew) were at the reunion. Family members came from as far away as California, Georgia, New York, North Carolina, South Carolina, and Texas, including several Chesnut descendants. Around 140 in all, according to the guest register.

133

At the family reunion in 1982, members posed for a photo on the steps of the house, including the two sons of Evans & Maud Haile (14th child of Thomas & Serena Haile): Thomas Evans Haile and James Graham Haile Sr. and their families.
Bottom step: (left to right) Jan Haile (Mrs. James Graham Haile Jr.), Angie Haile (daughter of James Graham Haile Jr. and Jan Haile), Leslie Parrish (Bev Parrish's daughter), Beverly Haile Parrish (daughter of James Graham Haile Sr. & Eloise Haile), Phil Parrish (Bev's husband)
Next step: (left to right) the woman with hands on Angie's shoulders is Eloise Smith Haile (the wife of James Graham Haile Sr) and James Graham Haile Sr. (son of Evans & Maud Haile)
On the next step (left to right): James Graham Haile Jr. (son of James Graham Haile Sr. & Eloise Haile), Allen Haile (son of James Graham Haile Jr. & Jan Haile), Thomas Evans Haile (son of Evans & Maud Haile), Nancy Haile Bowden (daughter of Thomas Evans Haile & Julia Jordan Haile), and Evans Haile (son of James Graham Haile Sr. and Eloise Haile)
The young man with the dark beard on the top row is John Bowden (the husband of Nancy Haile Bowden). The gray-haired man sitting on the railing on the left is M.A. Taylor, caretaker of the Homestead property since the 1970s and a man the Hailes called Toby Taylor. His granddaughter, Kaley Taylor Behl, is Secretary of the HHH Board of Directors and a docent at the HHH.

The National Register

The nomination form for National Register status was prepared by local historian Murray D. Laurie in May 1985. On May 2, 1986, the Homestead was placed on the National Register of Historic Places.

This plaque is on the wall of the house facing the front porch.

More about the Historic American Building Survey (HABS): From the report dated Spring 1986: "This project was undertaken as part of a course requirement for the Architecture Preservation Graduate option of the University of Florida, directed by Herschel Shepard, FAIA and Susan Tate, AIA. Documentation of the structure was begun in 1977 by John Bellamy, Sergio Gonzalez Jr,, E.J. March, and G. Allan Urda.

The documentation process has since been completed by Sharon Behan, Marta Cruz-Casse, Robert Delaune, Daniel Houston, and Rebecca Spain, as presented here." (This report was dated Spring 1986 and compiled by Sharon Behan, Marta Cruz-Casse, Robert Delaune, Daniel Houston, and Rebecca Spain.)

Among the structures that were not restored was the kitchen, pictured here in a 1926 photo. The kitchen was separated from the house in order to prevent the spread of any fire that might start in the kitchen. The kitchen, in fact, burned down some time after that. The site of the kitchen was determined from such photos and from the finding of the cornerstones and the hearth stones.

Today a sign indicates where the kitchen was located away from the house. A future project will be the construction of a replica kitchen.

Chapter Twenty-one: 1990 to 1999

This decade saw the restoration of the house.

Among the major developments of that decade were these: Thomas Evans Haile donated his half-interest to Alachua Conservation Trust (ACT). He passed away in 1993.

The Eloise S. Haile Revocable Trust was created by Graham Haile Sr.'s wife (Eloise) and their children: Graham Jr., Evans, and Beverly. They own the other half. There was a 99-year lease created between the Haile Trust and ACT. James Graham Sr. had passed away in 1984.

The 1990s would see a survey of the property and plans made for its restoration. Jay Reeves (who is currently on the HHH Inc. Board of Directors) was the architect in charge of the restoration, which took nearly five years to complete.

The care that the restoration experts took with the house can be seen even in the rear of the house, which is quite beautiful.

137

In June 1990, the Alachua Conservation Trust Inc. applied for a Historic Preservation Grant-In-Aid from the State of Florida in the amount of $470,000 for the full preservation of the Homestead. The proposed usage was for a house museum and office. Some of that grant request was funded.

In June 1992 a Plantation House and Site Utilization Study by Boykin-Hayter, Hall & Reeves Architects and Designers, P.A. was completed.

On October 2, 1992, Historic Haile Homestead Inc. (HHH Inc.) was created as a 501(c)3 non-profit organization whose mission is "the preservation, adaptive use, interpretation, and protection of the building and adjacent property known as the Haile Homestead in Alachua County, Florida for the use and enjoyment of the public and to educate the public as to the importance of preserving such historic places."

A pie safe used as a display case at the house has some of the artifacts found on the property during the archaeological study of the house and its environs.

In 1996 SouthArc Inc., owned by local archaeologists Martin Dickinson and Dr. Lucy Wayne, conducted an archaeological survey of the property. Among the artifacts found were plain whiteware and some ceramics, bottle glass, and cut and wire nails. The small amount of artifacts located may have been due to extensive looting over the years and/or that the Hailes carried off or buried their trash.

In 1996, the Haile family trust gave ACT a 99-year lease. ACT then partnered with HHH Inc., through another lease arrangement to allow HHH Inc. to operate the Homestead as house museum and tourist destination.

This page and the next several pages have photos of the deteriorating structure, prior to restoration.

DISINTEGRATING CHIMNEY BASE

COLUMN DAMAGE

FIREPLACE DAMAGE

PLASTER DAMAGE--NURSERY

UPSTAIRS CEILING DAMAGE

REPLACEMENT OF PIERS AND BEAMS

RESTORATION OF SHINGLE ROOF

Chapter Twenty-two: 2000 to 2009

The first two years of this decade saw the House being opened for tours in April 2001. Dr. Lucy Wayne and Martin Dickinson of RealSouth Tours were the original site managers, managing operations and coordinating the volunteer docent program. Under their leadership and guidance the opening of the Historic Haile Homestead as a house museum and tourist destination was successfully launched.

In December 2001 the Annual Homestead Holidays event was created and has become an annual Holiday tradition in Gainesville since. The docents decorate the house as the Hailes might have done it back in the 1800s. In 2006 another annual holiday event was added, the Candlelight Visits. This is the only time all year the Homestead is opened at night, under the glow of candlelight and soft lights.

The Nursery Room during a recent Candlelight Visit

143

In 2002 the Alachua Conservation Trust and HHH Inc. partnered to acquire a large grant from the County's Tourism Development Tax funds to build a Visitors' Center on the property. A major capital campaign was then initiated to raise the rest of the money to build an appropriate structure in which to greet visitors, house exhibits, operate a gift shop and host events.

The Allen & Ethel Graham Visitors' Center

In 2003 the Board of Directors of HHH Inc. took over operations and management of the docent program from RealSouth Tours.

In 2003 the first slave descendant tour took place at the House, bringing over 180 people from all parts of the country. The event received extensive coverage in the *Gainesville Sun.*

In celebration of 150 years, the State of Florida historical marker was unveiled on October 20, 2006 by Mike Castine (HHH & ACT), Karen Kirkman (HHH Inc. President), Evans Haile, Graham Haile, Ginger Childs (HHH), and Barbara Stringfellow (HHH) pictured in the photo below left to right. The marker, which was funded by the Alachua County Tourist Development Tax, was written by Karen Kirkman.

On that day, a cloudy, humid one, close to fifty people gathered along Archer Road to see the State of Florida historical marker unveiled. The unveiling ceremony was attended by Evans and Graham Haile, as well as descendants of the Kelley family.

These are the words on the plaque:

"Historic Haile Homestead at Kanapaha Plantation"

"One of the oldest houses in Alachua County, the Historic Haile Homestead was the home of Thomas Evans Haile, his wife Esther Serena Chesnut Haile and fourteen of their children. The Hailes came here from Camden, South Carolina in 1854 to establish a 1,500 acre Sea Island Cotton plantation which they named Kanapaha. Enslaved black craftsmen completed the 6,200 square foot manse in 1856. The 1860 census showed 66 slaves living here. The Hailes survived bankruptcy in 1868 and turned the property into a productive farm, growing a variety of fruits and vegetables including oranges."

[continued on next page]

The walkway to the house from the parking lot is very attractive.

"Serena Haile died in 1895; Thomas in 1896. The Homestead, which passed to son Evans, a prominent defense attorney, became the site of house parties attended by some of Gainesville's most distinguished citizens. The Hailes had the unusual habit of writing on the walls; all together over 12,500 words with the oldest writing dating to the 1850s. The Homestead was placed on the National Register of Historic Places in 1986. A restoration was completed in 1996. Still partly owned by descendants of Evans Haile, the Homestead is one of the few remaining homesteads built by Sea Island cotton planters in this part of Florida."

The walkway to the house is nicely shaded.

The Talking Walls

In April 2001 just before the Homestead opened for tours on a regular basis, docent-in-training Karen Kirkman (now HHH President and Historian) asked site manager Dr. Lucy Wayne if the walls had ever been documented. The answer of course was no. So after the Homestead opened, Kirkman, who was frequently on docent duty, spent six months going from room to room, wall to wall, writing down what others had written decades before. Another two months was spent typing it all into a Word file. The word count was over 12,500 words, not including art work.

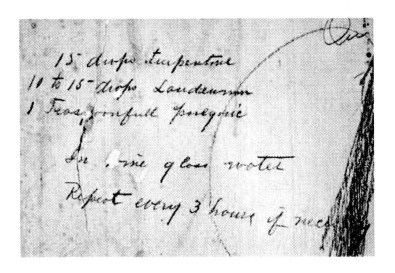

The east wall of the parlor has a medicinal recipe to cure dysentery, written by Serena Haile.

She found writing in almost every room and closet. What she discovered was not mindless "graffiti" as the wall writing was often characterized in the press. It was a record of life, right on the walls, with a general organization to it. The docents began to call them "Talking Walls" as they indeed tell a story.

The two front rooms, the public rooms, contained mostly "party day" writing from the early 1900s and later, after the house was no longer occupied. It is assumed that, in the rooms where visitors were entertained, the walls were bare.

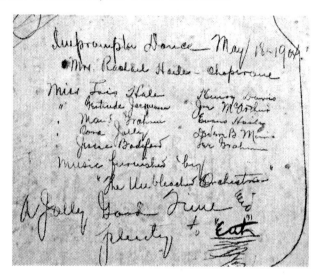

The south wall of the Music Room has mention
of an "Impromptu Dance" on May 18, 1904 -
the writing mentions an Unbleached Orchestra (see below).

One exception was a medicinal recipe next to a window in the Parlor in Serena Haile's handwriting. That remained a mystery until the Haile family reunion in May 2011. Descendants of Sydney Haile brought a picture of the Homestead with writing on the back – and the Parlor was identified as having been Serena's bedroom for a time. Along with lists of party goers in the early 1900s are references to the "Unbleached Orchestra." An article in the social column of the Gainesville newspaper revealed that the "orchestra" was comprised of a small group of African-Americans who played ragtime music for the parties at the old Haile house.

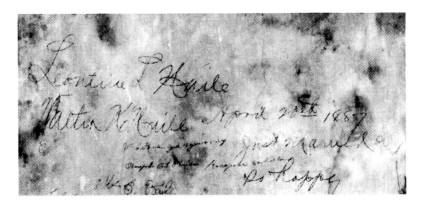

Sometimes the writing on the wall will commemorate
an important event, for example the wedding
of Walter Haile and Leontine Lockett (see Chapter Sixteen).

Upon entering the private rooms of the house, one can see that the character of the writing changes. It becomes older writing done by Haile family members.

Most of the writing in the Master Bedroom was done by Serena Haile herself: poetry, lists, household remedies, height charts of children and grandchildren, numbers of rats killed in the house, and in other rooms, a menu, inventories of linens, silverware and dishes, etc.

Writing in the two children's rooms upstairs was done by the children, of course. During the summer of 2013 a crack appeared in the plaster of a wall in the Plantation Office, a room in which Kirkman had previously found no writing.

Kirkman and HHH board member, architect Jay Reeves noticed pencil markings on the newly exposed plaster.

Reeves was able to determine that it was original plaster that had been covered up during the 1990s restoration. He suggested it would be alright to chip the new plaster off. One day Kirkman and HHH Secretary Kaley Behl chipped the new plaster off the wall using credit cards from their wallets.

What was revealed was amazing: very old writing from the 1860s through 1890s including a reference to a Company in the Confederate Army, the only reference to the War between the States found on the walls (see photo below).

It is likely more writing is yet to be found on the walls. Why they wrote on the walls to begin with is still a mystery, though it is likely a shortage of paper was the reason. Standing on the original heart pine floors in front of a piece of writing one can easily imagine the great fun and great sorrows that played out in the old Haile Homestead.

The Diary

After completing the documentation of the "Talking Walls," Karen Kirkman asked the site managers about a reference to Serena Haile's diary that she had seen in the docent manual. According to oral tradition, the diary had been split up among the children of Thomas and Serena Haile. One section went to family in Miami, one section to Jacksonville, and another section remained in Gainesville.

At some point the sections were reunited, likely when plans were made to open the house as a museum. After receiving permission to transcribe it, Kirkman spent the next several years putting the pieces in proper order and deciphering Serena Haile's writing. Abbreviations, use of nicknames, little to no punctuation, and incomplete sentences presented quite a challenge, and it became clear that the diary would not be understood without its historical context. Thus, years of research have followed.

An image that shows what a fragile condition the diary is in

Just when she thought the task was completed and the work ready for publication, Cameron Dow Gates, a descendant of Carol Matheson Haile, appeared at the Homestead one Saturday morning after she and her husband had driven over from St. Augustine. Kirkman happened to be standing in for another docent for a couple of hours that morning so she was thrilled to meet Mrs. Gates.

It wasn't long before Mrs. Gates said she had Serena's diary. Her father had passed away years before and she finally had gone through his belongings – and found a section of the diary. It didn't take long to realize that the portion of the diary in Mrs. Gates's possession contained some of the missing years. At the encouragement of Evans Haile, Mrs. Gates donated the diary portions to HHH Inc. She passed away suddenly a few months later.

Another view of the diary

Today the diary encompasses most of 1874 through 1893, with just a few gaps. Transcription of these "new" pages has been completed and research is on-going. Kirkman plans to publish the diary within the next few years. She is convinced there are more pieces out there, as the diary begins and ends in the middle of a week. She hopes that over time more pieces of the diary will begin to emerge from attics and basements – any piece, even a page, would be gratefully accepted.

The Historic Kanapaha Presbyterian Church

The historic 1886 Kanapaha Presbyterian Church continues to serve the community. In 2006 Memorial Fellowship Hall was constructed to serve the needs of the congregation and the community. The 4,200 square foot facility is available for weddings, receptions, banquets and meetings at reasonable rates. Kanapaha Presbyterian Church is the perfect spot for those seeking to incorporate history and tradition into their special events.

A large stained-glass window in the church - In the 1880s Serena Haile and other ladies of the congregation raised money to purchase these windows by selling ice cream from the back of wagons.

In 2008 site work for the Visitors' Center got under way. Brown & Cullen Inc. did the engineering work, while Commercial Industrial Corporation did the actual site work. At this point additional fundraising was required to go further.

Chapter Twenty-three: 2010 to 2014

In the spring of 2011 the Board of Directors of the Historic Haile Homestead decided it was time to have another Haile family reunion. A committee, headed by Bev Haile Parrish, granddaughter of Evans Haile, put together a splendid event. On May 7, 2011, the second Haile family reunion was held on the grounds of the Homestead.

Over 100 Haile, Chesnut, and other old Gainesville descendants from around the country were in attendance. A Sydney Haile descendant travelled all the way from Germany to be there. After a catered lunch and tours of the Homestead, the descendants were welcomed by Evans Haile (representing the descendants of Evans and Maud Haile), ACT Treasurer/HHH Vice President Mike Castine, and HHH President Karen Kirkman. The Vice Chair of the Board of County Commissioners for Alachua County, Paula Delaney, read a County proclamation honoring the Homestead's history. There was even a scanning station where descendants could either donate old pictures and letters or have them scanned for the Haile Archives.

155

By 2011 fundraising efforts met with success. In December 2011, the dried-in version of the Allen & Ethel Graham Visitors' Center opened (see photo below), restrooms only, thanks to a major naming gift from the family of Catherine Graham Minderman (1928-2010). Allen and Ethel Graham were the parents of Mrs. Minderman, and relatives of Maud Graham Haile. Joyner Construction was the builder, and Bill Warinner, the architect.

Other naming gifts had been received from Mr. Ron Gates to name the front porch of the Visitors Center "In loving memory of Louise Dupray Haile Dow, mother of Robert N. Dow Jr. and his daughter, Cameron Dow Gates"; from Nancy Haile Bowden to name the display/reception area "In loving memory of Thomas E. and Elizabeth J. Haile"; and from Mary Chesnut Budd Gearing to name the Breezeway "In loving memory of Mary Chesnut Haile Budd." The final phase of the Visitors' Center is expected to be completed by the end of 2014, by Art Middleton Construction.

The front of the Allen & Ethel Graham Visitors' Center with its sign

In 2012 a Tropical Storm Debbie dropped a record amount of rain on North Central Florida, which caused extensive leaking of the Homestead's roof. The roof had to be tarped to protect the Talking Walls inside the house. In May 2013 ACT had a new pine shake roof installed. This roof is expected to last fifty years.

In 2013 a matching grant from the Special Projects fund of the National Society of the Daughters of the American Revolution (DAR) was received, and the water damaged walls and ceilings were repaired.

Mourners in period costume at the Kanapaha Church Cemetery during the Heart, Home, and History Tour in February, 2014

In February 2013, Kanapaha Presbyterian Church part-nered with the Historic Haile Homestead to offer the Heart, Home & History Tour. The tour, which began at the Haile Homestead, moved to the Kanapaha Church Cemetery and concluded at the historic Kanapaha Presbyterian Church, was based largely upon the relationship between the Hailes and their beloved church, lifted from the pages of Serena Haile's diary. The tour has now become an annual February event and fundraiser.

Kanapaha Church Cemetery

The tranquil, historic Kanapaha Presbyterian Church Cemetery at the end of S.W. 63rd Blvd. off Archer Road is all that remains of the site of the original 1859 church. The earthly remains of some of the area's original settlers lay beneath the hallowed grounds of about 3.5 acres: the Haile family, Z.T. Taylor, Thomas G. Ramsey, J.D. Young, and W.F. Rice, to name a few.

Within the Haile family enclosure is the oldest dated burial, John Chesnut Haile, who died in January 1867. The grave with the earliest birth year belongs to Amelia Haile, Thomas Haile's mother, who lived from 1795 to 1880 (see image to the right).

Another person of distinction buried within the Haile enclosure is the Hailes' son-in-law, Robert Fenwick Taylor, who served on the Florida Supreme Court from 1891 to 1925, serving three terms as Chief Justice.

In the corner is the grave of Bennet Kelley (1844 – 1933), who was once enslaved by the Hailes. The cemetery survived a period of neglect and vandalism and, thanks to the efforts of the Rancourt family, Francis and Barbara Rea, Sarah Haynes, and others, is meticulously and lovingly cared for today by the congregation of Kanapaha Presbyterian Church.

Each year the cemetery is the site of Kanapaha Presbyterian Church's Easter Sunrise Service, to which all are welcomed.

In October 2013 ground penetrating radar (GPR) revealed at least 33 unmarked graves. This came as no surprise as Serena Haile mentioned several burials in the diary for which there are no grave markers today.

A mapping survey which merged the GPR data will help the congregation mark each of those graves with an "Unknown" granite marker.

HHH President Karen Kirkman and HHH Secretary Kaley Behl, who also serve as co-elders for Church History and Cemetery Management at Kanapaha Presbyterian Church, have spearheaded this effort.

Some parts of the cemetery have small walls around them.

The Military Grave Stone for Thomas E. Haile

Sunday, February 24th, 2013 seemed like the usual afternoon of tours at the Homestead, but it wouldn't stay that way. Two older folks came down the path with a hand cart, and on the cart was a large, dirty white rectangular stone.

Docents Anne Clayton and Matthew Ruppert couldn't believe what they heard when the couple began to speak. On the cart was a military grave stone for Thomas E. Haile.

The military grave stone for Thomas E. Haile -
the letters stand for the following: BVT = Brevet;
2d LT = Second Lieutenant; CO G = Company G;
5 BN FLA CAV = 5th Battalion Florida Cavalry

They said that someone else found the marker partially buried in a creek bed along Rattlesnake Creek, on the other side of Gainesville. That person gave them the marker and they decided to bring it home to the Homestead.

The couple refused to give their names. Anne excitedly called Karen Kirkman in North Carolina. Docent Kaley Behl moved the marker all by herself to Karen's garage for safe keeping; quite a feat since it weighs over 100 lbs.

Then the detective work began: for one thing the year of Thomas Haile's death was wrong. He died in 1896, just 20 minutes before the new year! What was the origin of the marker?

Descendants Graham Haile and Nancy Haile Bowden were contacted to see if they had any knowledge of when the marker was either ordered or stolen. We also put the question to the Homestead's Facebook fans, many of whom are Haile descendants. No one knew of the marker's existence, let alone its theft! Suffice it to say that the marker had to have been missing for decades! The marker does not appear in the Veterans Administration database of marker applications.

To deepen the mystery, the Register of Deceased Veterans for Alachua County compiled in 1941 lists Thomas Haile as a Private in Company G buried in Kanapaha Church cemetery. The death date shown was 1897, as was originally on this marker. To this day the origin of the marker is still a mystery. Graham Haile generously paid to have the year on the marker corrected by O.T. Davis Monument Company, which also cleaned up the stone.

On April 27, 2013, the Historic Haile Homestead and the Madison Starke Perry Camp #1424, Sons of Confederate Veterans rededicated the marker at the foot of Thomas Haile's grave in the Kanapaha Presbyterian Church Cemetery.

To the right is a photo of Thomas Haile's grave site in the Kanapaha Presbyterian Church Cemetery. Notice the military marker at the foot of the grave stone.

161

Recent News

In March 2014, the Daughters of the American Revolution erected a historical marker at the Homestead commemorating the founding of their chapter in 1922 by, among others, several nieces of Thomas and Serena Haile (see photo below). The event was attended by state and national DAR dignitaries, as well as the chair of the Board of County Commissioners for Alachua County.

In May 2014 word was received that a preservation grant submitted by ACT to the State of Florida Bureau of Historic Preservation Small Matching Grant program was funded. This important work will address termite protection, and window, shutter and plaster repair among other preservation issues.

Conclusion

Without a doubt the "Talking Walls" of the Historic Haile Homestead make this house extra special, unique, in fact. We know of no other historic house in the country which can claim over 12,500 words written on its walls. The writing spans decades, beginning in 1859 and, for the most part, ending in the 1930s.

The house has a story to tell: on its walls, in its architecture, on its grounds, and through historical research. It speaks of joys and sorrows of its owners and of the enslaved people who toiled in the fields and scrubbed its floors. Stories of birth and death; of wealth and poverty; of hand-hewn beams and milled siding; of laughter and tears.

The Homestead and its stories are ours to preserve and share. Once a hidden treasure known only to but a few, the Historic Haile Homestead, through the dedication and commitment of the Haile family, the Alachua Conservation Trust, and the board, docents, and members of Historic Haile Homestead Inc. is open for all to appreciate.

Appendix A: Genealogy of the Haile Family

HAILE

Benjamin Haile II, b. 1768 in VA, d. 1849, Camden, SC m. (1) Mary Cureton (1768-1810) in 1784
Children: Susan, James Cureton, Sarah, Catherine (married Christopher Matheson), and Benjamin III.
m. (2) Amelia White Evans, (b. 1795, d. Feb. 9, 1880 in Gainesville, FL) – married Aug. 11, 1811 at the age of 16, moved to Alachua County, FL in the 1850s.
The children: (* = moved to Florida)
Mary Haile, b. 1812, d. 1865 Camden, SC, married William Kennedy and lived in Camden.
Caroline Haile, b. 1814, d. 1888, Old Quaker Cemetery, Camden, unmarried
Rebecca Ann Haile, b. 1817, Camden, SC, m. Farquar Matheson, lived in Camden; d. 1848
Columbus Haile, b. 1820, Camden, SC, m. Louisa McCaa (sister of Elise Haile), (1825-1905); lived in Staunton, VA; d. 1892
Elizabeth Haile, b. 1822, Camden, SC; married Thomas E. Shannon (b. 1820, d. 1881) lived in Camden

*Thomas Evans Haile, May 31, 1824, Camden, SC, m. Esther Serena Chesnut (b. May 31, 1827, d. Dec 7, 1895) on March 13, 1847; d. Dec. 31, 1896; both buried in the Kanapaha Church Cemetery; 15 children;
*Edward Haile, b. 1827, d. 1903 in Atlanta, GA, buried in Linwood Cemetery, Columbus, GA; m. (1) Mary Whitaker Chesnut June 18, 1851 (b. 1830, d. 1858, buried in Old Quaker Cemetery, Camden, SC - sister of Serena Haile), two children m. (2)Warren "Warnie" Chapman
William Haile, b. 1830, d. 1849, buried in Old Quaker Cemetery, Camden, accidentally killed while a student at Univ. of Virginia
*John Haile, b. 1833, m. Amelia Gibbes, lived in Charleston, had property in Gainesville, FL; two children
*Charles Evans Haile, b. Dec 11, 1835, d. Aug 14, 1924; m. Elise Whitaker McCaa, moved to Gainesville, FL; eight children.

CHESNUT

John Chesnut, b. Dec 23, 1799, Camden, SC; eldest son of James Chesnut (b. Feb 19, 1773 in Camden, SC), owner of Mulberry Plantation, and Mary Bowes Cox (b. Mar. 22, 1775 in Trenton, Mercer Co, NJ); attended Princeton University, class of 1819, but did not graduate; m. Charlotte "Ellen" Whitaker, May 10, 1826 (b. Feb. 10, 1807, on the west side of the Wateree River near Camden, SC; her father was Thomas Whitaker; her mother was Mary Williams; d. Apr. 6, 1851, buried at Knight's Hill next to her husband); built Cool Spring Plantation in 1834; contracted measles during a brief military campaign in Florida (Second Seminole War) in 1836, and complications led to a serious lung condition; he traveled to various Sulphur Springs (Grey, Red and White) in Virginia with his brother James seeking to be cured. In May 1839 his father, James Chesnut Sr., sent him to France to consult with specialists sending his brother James along. He returned in September and consulted doctors in New York and Philadelphia; returned to Camden and died shortly thereafter in December, 1839 at Mulberry Plantation; buried at Knight's Hill next to his wife. His younger brother, James Chesnut, became a general in the Confederate Army, married Mary Boykin Miller, who wrote the famous *Diary from Dixie*.

Children:
*Esther Serena Chesnut; b. May 31, 1827, Camden, SC; d. Dec 7, 1895; m. Thomas Evans Haile, March 13, 1847
James Chesnut: b. May 23, 1828; d. about Dec. 23, 1829 at Camden, SC; buried at "Knight's Hill" burying ground, Camden, SC
Mary Whitaker Chesnut: b. July 10, 1830; d. May 14, 1858, m. Edward Haile (Thomas Haile's brother)
*Thomas Whitaker Chesnut: b. July 9, 1833 at old Knight's Hill place. m. Mary "Helen" Taylor, d. Apr 12, 1901
*James Chesnut: b. Feb 18, 1835 at Camden, SC; m. Amelia B. McCaa (sister of Elise Haile), d. Feb 15, 1916; moved to Alachua County in 1861

John Chesnut: b. July 15, 1837 at "Cool Spring"; d. June 15, 1868 at Aunt Sally Chesnut's residence "Bloomsbury" near Camden, "Johnny" as he was called was the "Cool Captain" mentioned frequently in Mary Chesnut's diaries.

Ellen Whitaker Chesnut: b. Mar 31, 1839 at Camden, SC; d. Dec 12, 1862 at the home of Thomas and Serena Haile; buried at Knight's Hill by her parents' side.

Children of Thomas and Serena Haile

1.   John Chesnut Haile: b. Jan. 14, 1848; d. Jan. 21, 1867
2.   Ellen Whitaker Haile: b. Mar. 28, 1849; d. July 27, 1850
3.   Amelia Evans Haile: b. Nov. 28, 1850; d. Nov. 26, 1901; m. Robert Fenwick Taylor (b. Mar. 10, 1849, d. Feb. 26, 1928); three children
4.   Benjamin Haile: b. Mar. 13, 1852, d, Oct. 10. 1889; m. Rachel Denton Haile; one child
5.   Thomas Evans Haile Jr.: b. Aug. 18 1853; d. Dec. 29, 1885
6.   James Chesnut Haile: b. June 29, 1855; d. May 9, 1891
7.   William Edward Haile: b. Feb. 10, 1857; d. Feb. 11, 1935; m. (1) Margaret "Maggie" B. Turnbull; one child; m. (2) Adele (Nonnie) Lawrence Tatum; two children
8.   Lawrence Whitaker Haile: b. July 15,1858; d. Sept. 25, 1945; m. (1) Olivia Sutherland Dawson, Dec. 27, 1887, double ceremony with George Reynolds Haile and Maggie Alston; children: two children; m.(2) Mary Louise Bauskett; two children
9.   Mary Chesnut Haile: b. Sept. 22, 1859; d. Aug. 15, 1938; m. Josiah T. Budd II; five children
10.   Charles Evans Haile: b. Jan. 11,1861; d. Jan. 3, 1934; m. Annie Morgan Hayes
11.   Walter Kennedy Haile: b. June 30, 1862; d. Mar. 20, 1920; m. Leontine Lockett; one child
12.   Sydney Haile: b. Oct.16, 1864; d. Dec. 12,1938; m. Natalie Venable; five children
13.   George Reynolds Haile: b. Dec. 20, 1865; d. Mar. 28, 1934; m. Margaret "Maggie" Ulmer Alston, Dec. 27, 1887, double wedding with Lawrence Whitaker and Olivia Sutherland Dawson Haile; five children   166

14.　Evans Haile: b. June 11, 1869; d. Dec. 3, 1934; m. Maud Graham; two children

15.　Carol Matheson Haile: b. Dec. 15, 1870; d. Aug. 18, 1955; m. Henrietta (Etta) Dupray; five children

Below is the Haile Family Tree

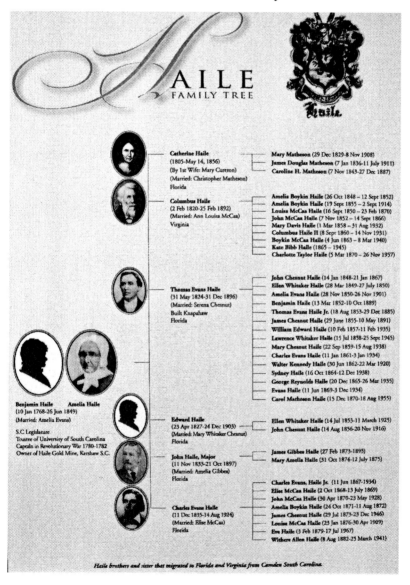

References

Adams, William Hampton. *Waverly Plantation: Ethnoarchaeology of a Tenant Farming Community.* Resource Analyst, Inc. Bloomington, IN. 1980

Alachua County Clerk of the Court. Ancient Records, www.clerk-alachua-fl.org/archive/default.cfm, Gainesville, FL.

Behan, Sharon, Marta Cruz-Cassé, Rob Delaune, Daniel Houston and Rebecca Spain. *Haile Plantation House.* College of Architecture, University of Florida, Gainesville, FL. 1986.

Behl, Kaley and Karen Kirkman, "Historic Kanapaha Presbyterian Church" (unpublished mss.).

Boykin-Hayter, Kennette and Jay Reeves. *Historic Haile Homestead: A Plantation House and Site Utilization Study.* Boykin-Hayter, Hall & Reeves, Gainesville, FL and Alachua Conservation Trust, Gainesville, FL. 1992 – .

Branton, Isaiah. Personal Communication. Interview with Karen Kirkman, HHH.

Conroy, Carollinda. *Southern Plantation.* Ms. On File, Alachua Conservation Trust. 1980 -2004.

Dickinson, Martin F. and Lucy B. Wayne. *Kanapaha Plantation: Archaeological Survey at the Haile House, Alachua County, Florida.* SouthArc, Inc., Gainesville, FL. 1996

Edward K. Eckert, "Contract Labor in Florida During Reconstruction," *Florida Historical Quarterly,* vol.,1968, pp. 34-51.

Edwards, Jay D. and Tom Wells. *Historic Louisiana Nails: Aids to Dating of Old Buildings.* Geoscience Publications, Louisiana State University, Baton Rouge, LA, 1993

Ferguson, Leland. *Uncommon Ground: Archaeology and Early African America 1650-1800.* Smithsonian Institution Press, Washington, DC. 1992,

Gannon, Michael. *The Cross in the Sand: The Early Catholic Church in Florida, 1513-1870.* Gainesville: University Press of Florida, 1965.

Gates, William C., Jr. and Dana E. Ormerod. "The East Liverpool Pottery District: Identification of Manufacturers and Marks." *Historical Archaeology*, 16 (1-2), 1982.

Gowan, Sam. "The Haile Place." *Historic Gainesville*, VI (3). 1977a.

– "The Haile Place. 1855 to the present." *Historic Gainesville*, VI (4). 1977b.

Haile, Evans. "Personal communication." Great-grandson of Thomas Haile. 1997.

Haile, Serena. Personal journal transcribed and researched by Karen A. Kirkman, 1874-1893, Gainesville, FL (2003-present).

Haile, Thomas. Personal communication, Haile family member. Map and comments in *Historic Haile Homestead: A Plantation House and Site Utilization Study*, Boykin-Hayter, Hall & Reeves, Gainesville, FL and Alachua Conservation Trust, Gainesville, FL. 1992.

Hildreth, Charles H. and Merlin G. Cox. *History of Gainesville, Florida 1854-1979.* Alachua County Historical Society, Gainesville, FL. 1981.

Jones, John Paul. "Alachua County's Unknown Treasure." *Florida Living*, August, 1991:52-54.

Jones, John Paul. Interview with L. B. Wayne, SouthArc, Inc., Gainesville, FL. 1996.

Kennedy, Wm. T., editor-in-chief. *History of Lake County, Florida. Part II, Biographical. Sketches of Leading Citizens of Lake County, Florida*: Tavares, Fla: Lake County Historical Society, 1988, pp. 221-222: for information about William "Willie" Edward Haile.

Kirkland, Thomas J. and Robert M. Kennedy. *Historic Camden: Part One: Colonial and Revolutionary*, publ. 1905; *Part Two: Nineteenth Century*, publ. 1926. Camden, SC: The Kershaw County Historical Society. Reprinted 1994.

Kirkman, Karen. Transcription of the Talking Walls of the Historic Haile Homestead. 2001.

Kirkman, Karen. *Wit & Wisdom of the Talking Walls*. Gainesville, FL. 2002.

Laurie, Murray D. *National Register of Historic Places Nomination Proposal – Florida, Haile Homestead*. Historian, Gainesville, FL. 1985.

McCormick, Fenwick Donald. *Planters, Plantations & Presbyterians: Kanapaha & Reverend W.J. McCormick*. Ocala, FL: Fenwick Enterprises, 2001?

Morris, Allen. *Florida Place Names*. Sarasota, FL: Pineapple Press, 1995.

Muhlenfeld, Elisabeth. *Mary Boykin Chesnut: A Biography*. Baton Rouge, LA.: Louisiana State University Press, 1981.

Pettus, Louise. "Haile Gold Mine." http://www.rootsweb.ancestry.com/~sclancas/history/hailegoldmine.htm

Raymond, Robert. Newspaper article on Haile gold mine, Camden, SC. On file, Alachua Conservation Trust, Gainesville, FL. n.d.

Reeves, Jay. "Personal communication," architect, Jay Reeves and Associates, Gainesville, FL. 1996.

Shofner, Jerrell H. "Florida in the Balance: The Electoral Count of 1876," *The Florida Historical Quarterly*, vol. 47, no. 2 (Oct., 1968), pp. 122-150.

Toulouse, Julian Harrison. *Bottle Makers and Their Marks*. New York: Thomas Nelson, Inc., 1971.

U.S. Department of Agriculture (USDA). Aerial photographs, Alachua County. Map Library, University of Florida, Gainesville, FL. 1937.

U.S. Geological Survey (USGS). Arredondo, FL, 15-minute topographic quadrangle map. 1890.

Photo credits

The following abbreviations are used for the list of photo credits: EH = Evans Haile, FM = Florida Memory Collection at the Florida State Archives in Tallahassee, HC = Hank Conner, HHHA = Historic Haile Homestead Archives, KK = Karen Kirkman, KM = Kevin McCarthy, KPC = Kanapaha Presbyterian Church.

Front cover: Mike Kirkman; i-ii: KM; 1-2: FM; 3: KM; 4 (both): FM; 5: Lillian C. Buttre (1858-1881). American Portrait Gallery from Wikimedia Commons; 6: Captain Samual Eastman - National Library of Medicine. Licensed under Public domain via Wikimedia Commons; 7-11: FM; 12: KM; 13-14: FM; 15: KM; 16: KK; 17 (TOP): Cheraw Spectator; 17 (BOTTOM): Camden Journal; 18: KK; 19: FM; 20: KK from a postcard picture in her collection; 21-23: FM; 24: KK; 25: EH; 26 (both): HHHA; 27: FM; 28: EH; 29: KK; 30: KM; 31: HC; 32-33: KM; 34: courtesy of Kanapaha Pres. Church and EH; 35: KM; 36: courtesy Boykin-Hayter, Hall & Reeves, Architects & Designers, P.A. and Alachua Conservation Trust; 37-44: KM; 45-47: FM; 48: KK; 49: KK; 50: KM; 51: EH; 52: KM; 53-54: FM; 55-57: HHHA/H. Vinson; 58: FM; 59: HHHA/C. Gearing; 60-61: HHHA; 62 (TOP): KK; 62 (BOTTOM): EH; 63: HHHA/C. Gearing; 64: KK; 65 (BOTH): KPC; 66: HHHA; 67: HC; 68: KK; 69: KM (TOP); 70 (BOTTOM): EH; 70: KK; 71-72: FM; 73: EH; 74-80: 81: EH; 82 (TOP): HHHA; 82 (BOTTOM): Alachua County Ancient Records – Marriage Book A, p. 775; 83: HHHA; 85-86: KM; 87: HHHA; 88: KK; 89: KM; 90 (all): FM; 91: HHHA; 92 (both): FM; 93: KK; 94 (TOP): FM; 94 (BOTTOM): HHHA; 95-96 (ALL): HHHA: EH; 97-99 (all): EH; 100 (BOTH): KK; 100 (BOTH): KK; 101 (both): HHHA; 102-04 (all): KM; 105: KK; 106: HHHA;107: HHHA/C. Gearing; 107-09: HHHA; 110-111: EH; 112: KM; 113-14: EH; 115: HHHA/Sydney Haile descendants; 116: HHHA; 117: HHHA/ Sydney Haile descendants; 118: Jay Reeves; 119-20: FM; 121: EH; 122-23: HHHA; 124: EH; 125: HHHA; 126-27: KK; 128: HHHA; 129-34: EH; 135: KM; 136 (TOP): HHHA; 136 (BOTTOM)-38: KM; 139-42 (all): Jay Reeves; 143-44: KK; 145: Mike Kirkman; 146-47: KM; 148-53: KK; 154: HC; 155-56: KM; : KM; 157: KK; 158-59: KM: 160: KK; 161-63: KM; 167: KM; 171-72: HC; 180: KM; back cover: HC.

About the authors

Karen Kirkman is President and Historian of Historic Haile Homestead Inc., has served on the Alachua County Historical Commission since 2006 and has researched and written four state historical markers in Alachua County. As co-elder for Church History & Cemetery Management at Kanapaha Presbyterian Church, she continues to research and document the Kanapaha Presbyterian Church Cemetery.

She is a member of the Alachua County Virtual Cemetery Project team and is a volunteer transcriber of Alachua County's Ancient Records, having transcribed almost 7,500 pages. In 2001 Karen documented the "Talking Walls" of the Historic Haile Homestead, and, over the past ten years, has been working on the transcription of Serena Haile's diary.

A native of central New York, Karen received her bachelor's degree from Eckerd College in 1976. In June 2012, after 35 years, she retired from the University of Florida, where she was an administrative faculty member and Director of Finance and Personnel in the College of Engineering until moving to the CFO's Office in July 2009. Karen has been married to Mike Kirkman, a retired high school math teacher and basketball coach, since 1976. They have two sons, Nate and Ryan, and an orange tabby cat named Bennet.

Kevin McCarthy earned his B.A. in American Literature from LaSalle College in 1963, his M.A. in English from the University of North Carolina – Chapel Hill in 1966 and his Ph.D. in Linguistics from the same school in 1970.

He taught in the Peace Corps in Turkey for two years, in Lebanon as a Fulbright Professor for one year, in Saudi Arabia as a Fulbright Professor for two years, and as a professor of English and Linguistics at the University of Florida for 33 years.

He has had 60 books published, mostly about Florida, plus 43 articles in scholarly and popular journals and has given over 300 talks to schools and academic groups.

In 2003 the University of Florida named him its Distinguished Alumni Professor. Since retiring from the University of Florida in 2005, he has taught writing workshops in Hanoi, Vietnam two times, and has taught English-as-a-Foreign Language in Spain four times.

He continues to research and write nonfiction books. For images of his book covers, see his web site: kevinmccarthy.us. He and his wife, Karelisa Hartigan, have five children between them.

INDEX

This index does not include Appendix A: Genealogy of the Haile Family